The Real
Secrets of the Top 20%

Praise for The Real Secrets of the Top 20%

"Inside selling requires a special talent - instant rapport, believability, and a few secret ingredients to create a buying atmosphere. All these elements are revealed in easy-to-master details within Mike Brooks's new book *The Real Secrets of the Top 20%*. If you master the secrets of the top 20%, you'll soon find yourself in the top 5%."

- **Jeffrey Gitomer**, author of *The Little Red Book of Selling*

"Decide today to reap the rewards of the top 20% of salespeople by reading and applying the great ideas in this book!"

- **Brian Tracy,** author of *Eat That Frog*

"Stop ad-libbing your way through your sales career. After reading this book, you'll be prepared for virtually any sales situation you encounter on the phone. Mike Brooks knows what it takes to succeed in inside sales."

- **Jill Konrath**, author of *Selling to Big Companies*

"Mike Brooks has hit a home run with *The Real Secrets of the Top 20%*. This must read book is perfect for anyone who works in the sales profession, and it is destined to become a classic."

- **Jeb Blount,** author of *PowerPrinciples*

"Mike Brooks has crafted an excellent resource for inside sales reps. He shares what it takes to be in the top 20% and stay there. This book is full of practical, easy to read advice and should be mandatory reading for anyone selling over the phone."

- **Clayton Shold,** President of Salesopedia

"Mr Inside Sales, Mike Brooks, hits the nail on the head in his book, *The Real Secrets of the Top 20%*. There is no baloney and no fluff in this straight forward book that tells it like it is. This is a must have book for those that want to start producing like a real Superstar!"

> **- Nick Moreno**, Head Sales Coach,
> The National Sales Center

"This is one of the best new books on inside sales in the last 25 years. In fact, it's so good it is the first time I've ever recommended another Sales Trainer's product! Mike Brooks explains, word-for-word, how he achieved Super Stardom in record time and how you can vault yourself into the Top 20% in your office, in your company, and yes, even in your industry, and double your income in record breaking time."

> **- Stan Billue**, CSP a.k.a. Mr. Fantastic

"When Juran named his principle after good old Vilfredo Pareto all those years ago, he could never have imagined that it would be re-named the "80/20 Rule" and applied to so many aspects of our commercial lives, particularly within the sales arena. Mike Brooks thoroughly understands the principle and in this, his latest book, outlines how to successfully apply it in order to become a Top 20% producer. It is an excellent piece of writing, which will benefit sales apprentices and seasoned professionals alike."

> **- Jonathan Farrington**, CEO of Top Sales Associates

Praise for The Real Secrets of the Top 20%

"Three gems unearthed in this book: 5 key scripts you simply must have; a candid perspective on the majority of sales pipelines; and important reminders about the steps to success. When you have the opportunity to learn from the person who wants to cut years off of your learning curve, you just can't help but want to jump in with both feet! There is one discussion Mike has with his readers that is worth the price of the book - exponentially - and that is, what 15 minutes can cost you and what you can gain in the amount of time the majority of your colleagues will unwittingly throw away!"

- **Leslie Buterin**, President of Top Dog Consulting

"Mike Brooks, Mr Inside Sales, brings us the tools and the proven techniques we need in his new book, *The Real Secrets of the Top 20%*. When using the telephone, our ability to communicate is less than 50% of what it is face-to-face. Mike has built a wondrous system to help us overcome this deficit and sell as well as we could "belly-to-belly." Maybe even better. I'm putting my order in now, and if you have the sense God gave a goose, you'll get one too."

- **Hank Trisler**, author of *No Bull Selling*

"Put down your phone and read this book! Mike Brooks will guide you into the elite 20% sales class. His telesales methodology is easily understood, and equally important, easily implemented. Read it and thrive!"

- **Lee B. Salz**, author of
Soar Despite Your Dodo Sales Manager

Praise for The Real Secrets of the Top 20%

"This is a must read for one simple reason: the only people who make it long-term in sales are those in the top 20%. If you're going to learn how to either become a top performer or remain a top performer, then you need to learn from someone who is. Mike is a top performer, and in this book he explains what it takes to be the top performer you want to be."

- Mark Hunter, The Sales Hunter

"There's no longer an excuse for whining about long hours and short paychecks when selling by telephone. Mike's breakthrough book will guide you into the ranks of the Top 20% of sales professionals and show you how to double your income! Why not YOU in the top 20%? And why not NOW? The road map is in your hands."

- Dave Anderson, author of
If You Don't Make Waves You'll Drown

"Without a doubt one of the best books on sales techniques I've read in years. Practical, proven techniques that don't sound made up or phony. Just real, straight forward advice that works! Buy this book today, and smile all the way to the bank!"

- Rick Frishman, co-author of *Where's Your Wow?*

"Why do most salespeople fail or just barely make it? Because they haven't learned and mastered the skills and behaviors that really work. Mike Brooks filters out the chaff and presents the strategies and tactics that can take you from where you are to the top of your company."

- Paul McCord, author of *SuperStar Selling*

Praise for The Real Secrets of the Top 20%

"Virtually every sales person I talk to wants to increase their sales and make more money. The problem is that many don't know how to achieve this. Mike Brooks has simplified the process. He offers practical, down-to-earth strategies that will skyrocket your sales - FAST! Make sure you read this book before your competitors find out about it!"

- **Kelley Robertson**, author of
The Secrets of Power Selling

"Finally the definitive book of phone techniques that REALLY WORK! If you use the telephone for setting appointments, qualifying prospects, or closing sales I believe Mike's book, *The Real Secrets of the Top 20%*, will show you how to do it better, faster, with less rejection, and, most importantly, put more money in your pocket!"

- **Joe Heller**, President of Trust Cycle Selling

"If you do inside sales or prospecting, you will get specific what-to-say techniques in this book that will help you avoid no's and put money in your pocket. It's a must-have for your sales library."

- **Art Sobczak**, Publisher of
Telephone Prospecting and Selling

"Read this book twice, first to understand all of the top 20% sales concepts and then again to memorize all of the sales scripts. These scripts will put money in your pocket. This is the book that you need to join the elite, top 20%."

- **Wendy Weiss**, The Queen of Cold Calling,
author of *Cold Calling for Women*

The Real Secrets
of the Top 20%

How To Double Your Income Selling Over The Phone

Mike Brooks,
Mr Inside Sales

Cape Coral, Florida

Sales Gravy Press
The Sales Book Publisher™
1726 SE 44th Terrace
Cape Coral, Florida 33904

Published by Sales Gravy Press
Printed in the United States of America

Cover Design: Dave Blaker
http://www.daveblaker.com

First Edition

Library of Congress Control Number: 2008929613

ISBN-13: 978-0-9794416-2-2
ISBN-10: 0-9794416-2-5

To my first sales manager, Peter Brooks, my brother, who taught me the first real secret of closing: *Listen and Think B-4 Responding.* Your encouragement, patience and example continue to inspire me.

Table of Contents

Start Here - I Mean It!
xv

The 80/20 Rule
Page 1

Prepare To Win
Page 9

**You Can't Close An
Unqualified Prospect**
Page 29

Getting To Closed
Page 61

The Objection
Page 89

Expect To Win
Page 105

**Bonus:
The Next Level**
Page 119

About the Author
Page 129

Acknowledgements
Page 131

Start Here - I Mean it!

First of all, congratulations! If you are holding this book in your hands it means that you have either: A) already bought the book and are at home diligently reading it (the best option, good for you!), or B) you are standing at the bookstore reading this and wondering if the material in this book applies to you. *Hint:* if you sell any product or service over the telephone, cold call, or set appointments, the information in this book applies to you. In fact, if you are in sales - *in any role* - this book will help you become your best. Proceed to the nearest checkout counter, buy it, go home and begin diligently studying it.

But let's say you have already bought this book and are now reading it. Then congratulations! You are doing something right now that 80% of salespeople never do, and that is investing time, money and energy in learning how to be the best. This is the first step to becoming a top 20% producer.

The second step to becoming a top 20% producer is to actually apply the information, tips, strategies, techniques, and scripts you find in this book. Once you begin doing that, you will see your sales and your income start to skyrocket.

Here is the best news of all. When you become a top 20% producer it means you start enjoying all of the bonuses, the perks, the income and lifestyle that top 20% sales professionals in all industries are already enjoying right now. That means the quiet confidence top producers have, and the financial security that allows them to spend more time with family and friends. It also means material things like homes and cars, and exciting travel and all the other things you dream about. Top 20% sales professionals use their talent and skill to make their dreams come true. This book is designed to teach you everything you need to know to go from where you are to where you want to be.

I'm excited for you. The reason I'm excited is I know

it is possible because I have done it! Over the last 25 years I have taught thousands of sales professionals how to move into the top 20%, and the good news (you'll find I'm full of good news) is that it is not that hard. In fact, being a bottom 80% producer is what is really hard.

Once you learn these skills and techniques and get into the habit of using them, you will find that being a top 20% producer is REALLY easy. This book is designed to show you, step-by-step, exactly how to do that. So congratulations, and let's get started.

- **Mike Brooks**, Mr Inside Sales

1 | The 80/20 Rule

My entire sales philosophy and training is based on the 80/20 rule in sales. If you've been in sales for any length of time, then I know you are familiar with it:

80% of the sales revenue and income in any company or industry is usually made by the top 20% of the sales force.

I know this is true for your sales organization as well. Can you name the top sales reps who work for your company? They are probably easy to identify. I've been selling products and services and training sales reps for 25 years, and everywhere I go it's always the same. The top 20% make 80% or more of the sales and income. It doesn't matter the industry, the product, or the service.

An important question

If all sales reps are selling the same product, working the same leads, have access to the same training materials and company literature, then what's going on? Why such a big difference? Why do some sales professionals do so well while the vast majority struggle and hate their jobs? *More importantly*, what can you begin doing right now to move into the top 20%, or into the top 5% of the top 20%?

Here's the good news: everything it takes to move into the top 20% - all the skills, techniques, methods and strategies - can be identified, learned, and applied. If you just do what the top 20% do, you will move into that elite group of top sales professionals. These skills and techniques have not only worked for me, but have worked for every sales professional who has committed to learning and using them.

How motivated are you to be the best? How much do you REALLY want to make the kind of money the top 20% make? Do you really want to buy the house of your dreams? Drive the car you wish you had? Have real peace of mind? You can! It is important to understand that if someone else can do it, you can do it better. Make this your mantra - *everywhere, everyday, in every situation.*

> **Make this your mantra:**
> **"If someone else can do it, I can do it better."**

You can study harder, apply yourself more, work smarter (and harder), use better qualifying techniques, learn to listen better, and close more business. The bottom line is if you apply these techniques, you can double or even triple your income selling over the phone.

How I Became a Top 20% Producer

I know all about the 80/20 rule in sales because I have been on both sides of it. I especially know how frustrating it is to be in the bottom 80%. I remember very clearly what it's like to be blown off on cold calls, to be frustrated by objections, to not know how to qualify leads, and to have my calls ignored. I know what it is like to struggle every month to have enough money and what it's like to hate sales. I also know what it's like to be a top 20% producer. It is one of the greatest feelings in the world. For me, it all started on *bonus day*.

Early in my career I worked at an investment banking company. At this company we celebrated bonus day at the end of each month. On bonus day all 25 sales reps got together in the conference room, and the president and sales manager would hand out awards to the top three producers of that month. This particular month, like the previous month, and the month before that, the top three awards went to the same top three sales professionals. I remember thinking, "What are they doing that I'm not doing? Why do *they* always win the awards?"

Later that day I had an important close to make. I was calling a prospect who always invested in one unit of every partnership we offered. I desperately needed this sale to make my rent for that month. With everything riding on this one sale I made the call. As soon as he answered the phone I could tell by his tone of voice that I was in trouble. He said that he had reviewed the material and decided that he would pass on this one, and with that, he hung up!

I was devastated. All of my bills flashed before my eyes. It felt like my life was over. I clearly remember getting up from my desk, walking out the front door like a zombie, and starting what would turn out to be a two mile walk in the blazing sun. Many thoughts raced through my mind but the predominant one was that I *hated* sales, and I was going to quit.

I started reviewing my life. I thought about my decision not to pursue my graduate degree. I thought about all of the things I could have been doing if only I had made better choices. I thought about how much I hated clients, hated objections, and hated having to depend on commission to scrape by every month.

Halfway into my walk, I made the decision to quit. I was through. But on my return to the office, a second thought occurred to me. If I quit now as a loser, I would probably quit again when the going got tough in another job. I don't know where that thought came from, but there it was.

Then I made a bargain with myself. I would give myself permission to quit sales - but only after I was a top producer. This idea really appealed to me because if I quit after I became a top producer, I could go out on top without guilt or shame. So to be honest, my motivation for becoming a top producer was that I could quit sales altogether. A little backwards I know, but that was a strong motivator for me, and I was committed.

As I finished my walk I had clarity. I committed at that very moment to buying and studying everything I could get my hands on to become a top producer in sales. It was at that moment I developed the mantra that if these other three top producers could do it then I could do it better! I committed to working harder, working smarter, and improving on every call.

Over the next 90 days I did everything I write about in this book. I bought an audio program on telemarketing skills and listened to it on the way to work and all the way home from work. I began recording my calls and critiquing them ruthlessly to improve what I said and how I said it. I wrote scripts and qualifying checklists. I learned how to disqualify prospects rather than spending time with people who were never going to buy. I created positive affirmation cards and began visualizing myself as a top producer.

Three months later we all gathered in that same conference room for *bonus day*. The president and sales manager were at the head of the room. As they got ready to announce the awards I could see one of the perennial top producers getting ready to jump out of his chair. But as the sales manager announced the name *Mike Brooks*, as closer of the month, I was the one who sprang out of my chair to receive my first sales award!

Everyone in the room was stunned except me. As I walked back to my chair with my award and check for $1000, I answered the amazed looks from the other sales reps by saying, *"That's right, and you just wait until next month!"*

By the end of that year I was not only the top closer of that office, but I was also the top closer out of five branch offices in Southern California. I won the trip to Hawaii, the Corvette convertible, and I bought my first home. I had discovered the secrets of top 20% performance, I'm here to tell you that it's a lot easier doing things the right way.

I did it and you can do it too

I guarantee that if you make the same commitment and take the same actions, *you will* get the same results. I can say this with complete confidence because I have taught these techniques to salespeople just like you. Those who made the commitment to use the skills, techniques, and strategies in this book all achieved the same top 20% results.

The real secret of top 20% performance is that there is no secret. You're either doing the things that will make you successful, or you are not. The top 20% do and say the same things no matter what they are selling, while the bottom 80% keep making the same old mistakes and getting the same poor results. You have a choice, right now, to change your life, and to become a top 20% producer. If you are willing to make a commitment, I'll show you how to do it. Let's get started!

> These techniques work! You can double or even triple your income.

5

Real Secrets

- **The top 20% make 80% of the sales and income in their companies and industries.**

- **You become a top 20% producer by learning and applying the proven skills and techniques in this book.**

- **If someone else can do it, you can do it better.**

- **It starts with a commitment to do whatever it takes to become the best.**

- **Succeeding in the top 20% is easier than struggling in the bottom 80%.**

- **Once you become a top 20% producer your whole life will change.**

- **The choice is yours to make.**

2 | *Prepare To Win*

Alexander Graham Bell once said, "Before anything else, preparation is the key to success." It is a fact that the top 20% spend more time in preparation than the bottom 80%. In this chapter you will learn the *seven* rules of the top 20%.

Becoming a top 20% producer starts with one thing - making a commitment to being the best.

Rule #1: Make a Commitment

I challenge you right here, right now, to commit to doing whatever it takes to become a top 20% producer. There's nothing more powerful than this commitment. When you commit, you will be amazed at how your life will change. Imagine what it will feel like to double or triple your income selling over the phone. Imagine how it will feel to finally be financially secure. Imagine how it will feel to have the professional respect you deserve, and the confidence of knowing that you will be a top producer wherever you go. Imagine moving into your new home or funding your retirement plan and building a secure future. Imagine living the life of a top sales professional.

Become a sales professional

First, stop thinking about having a job, and start treating your career as a profession. You are not a salesperson; you are a *sales professional*.

The profession of sales is one of the most lucrative careers in business today. Top sales professionals make more money than doctors, lawyers and nearly any other business professional.

When you start treating your career as a true profession, suddenly you become more willing to do the hard work required to be the best. Professionals take their careers seriously and don't mind investing their time, energy, and money into improving because it pays off big time.

Come in early and stay late

I know, I know, you hate this idea, but every professional is willing to put in the time it takes to be the best. Top results are not possible without top effort, so you should be prepared to come in early and to stay late. I remember the benefits I got from coming in early. While most of the sales reps got in at 9:00 am, I got in at 7:45 am. By the time they finally got on the phones I had already made over 50 calls! While they spent time at the coffee machine eating donuts and gossiping, I had already closed my first sale.

> Stop thinking about having a job, and start treating your career as a profession.

Staying late also has big benefits. The most important action I took at the end of each day was to get completely prepared for the next day. This meant organizing my leads, preparing my closes, and reviewing and setting priorities. Because I was prepared in advance, the next morning I was ready to jump on the phones rather than wasting valuable time shuffling leads and paperwork.

Sales Professionals...

- are the highest paid professionals in business;
- are more challenged and happier in their jobs;
- have more freedom and more flexibility;
- have more control of their income and goals;
- reap all of the rewards: recognition, trips, cash.

www.SalesGravy.com

The bottom line is that part of your commitment to become a top 20% producer means maximizing and prioritizing the time you spend at the office.

Manage your time

How are you with time management? Do you find yourself being driven by voice mails and e-mails rather than controlling your time during the day? The top 20% are fanatical about time management.

Unfortunately, we don't have room within the scope of this book to provide a detailed course in time management techniques. However, there are many great resources available to help you with time management. There are literally hundreds of articles, books, videos, and audio programs on the subject. You will find a list of my recommended favorites at *www.mrinsidesales.com/SecretResources.*

One of the most important principles I have learned about time management is the concept of priorities. To make an instant improvement in the way you manage your time, simply write three priorities for your day and commit to working each one to conclusion *before* moving to the next. In other words, avoid the temptation to multi-task.

This may sound like a simple idea, but you will be amazed by how effective it is. You will also be shocked by how much more you will get done. By identifying and working on the most important tasks, and focusing on each one to completion, you will be miles ahead of your competition.

You've no doubt heard the saying that we all have the same 24 hours in each day. The difference between the top 20% and the bottom 80% is simply how those 24 hours are used. To be in the top 20% you must learn to manage your time effectively.

Learn and practice effective techniques

One of the biggest mistakes the bottom 80% make is

ad-libbing their way through the sales day. The top 20% are successful because they are prepared in advance. They are prepared with effective scripts, techniques, and skills that work. This is why it is easy for them to be successful. The top 20% don't struggle.

This book is packed with effective and proven techniques for identifying, qualifying, and closing sales. If you learn and use these techniques you *will* be successful. These techniques work! They will get you in front of qualified prospects, move you past objections, and help you close more sales. When you use the right techniques and skills, you get the right results. It's as simple as that.

> One of the biggest mistakes the bottom 80% make is ad-libbing their way through the sales day.

Invest in yourself

Top 20% producers invest in themselves. They are constantly learning and growing as sales professionals. They subscribe to sales ezines, read books, listen to audio programs, and attend workshops. They do everything they can to improve their craft.

What can you do today to improve how you sell your product or service? What can you do to grow as a sales professional? Is there a sales conference you can attend? Are there sales trainers giving seminars in your city? Are there webinars or teleseminars you can attend? How about new books or audio programs on sales techniques? Have you checked out free sales podcasts and articles on the web?

You will find a list of resources at *www.mrinsidesales. com/SecretResources.*

Improve your product knowledge

Can you confidently answer all the questions your

prospects ask about your products or services? How about the most common questions? As a sales professional, you must know your product inside and out, and be prepared for the questions your prospects ask you.

Most of your competition is ad-libbing and often just making up answers. This makes them look foolish. The top 20%, on the other hand, not only know their products and services, but they know how to use this information to help close sales.

Make a list of ten to twenty questions your prospects ask, or are likely to ask, about your products or services. Then research and practice getting comfortable with the answers a little at a time during lunch, on breaks, or after work. At the same time develop powerful follow up questions to attach to your answers. Knowledge truly is power, and the more you know, the more confident you will become and the more sales you will close.

Develop an expectant attitude of success

The top 20% expect to succeed. They have a high confidence level that their prospects can feel over the telephone, because they know that people love to buy from confident sales professionals. You are going to learn how to develop a successful attitude in the last chapter, however, don't wait to get started. Ask yourself right now, *"Can I do what the top 20% in my company do?"* The answer is yes! And that yes is the beginning of a successful attitude.

> Knowledge is power. The more you know about your products and services, the more sales you will close.

Commit to working on your attitude by paying attention to and changing your self-talk. Find out what being a top 20% producer means in your organization. Discover what top 20% sales professionals produce in terms of sales volume and income. Make that your personal goal. Start by answering these questions:

- *What do the top producers make in my company or industry?*
- *What would it mean to me if I began making that kind of income?*
- *How will my lifestyle change?*
- *Will I be happier? What would that feel like?*
- *Am I ready for my life to change?*

These are questions you need to answer today. Once you've determined exactly how much money you will be making, and the kind of life you will be living, write that down and begin visualizing it as if it has already happened. This is the key to changing your beliefs.

With your new goal in hand, take a moment to write down how much money you expect to make this month and post it above your computer, or in your workstation. Get clear on how many deals you need to close to achieve your goal. Take out another sheet of paper and put in spaces for these deals or client names and number them. Leave them blank and begin filling them in as you close these deals. This will reinforce the progress you are making as you fill in blanks with each new deal you close. Expect success, you deserve it!

Rule #2: Practice Perfection

Practice doesn't make perfect. Practice only makes permanent. The problem is that the bottom 80% practice the wrong techniques day in and day out. And guess what happens? They get real good at doing the wrong things. This is one of the big reasons they are in the bottom 80%.

This is also why it is crucially important to learn from each call and practice the skills and techniques in this book. You see, each call is an opportunity to improve. Get into the habit right now of doing mini critique sessions after each call and commit to improving on the next one. After completing a call you should immediately ask yourself the following questions:

- *What went right?*
- *What should I change?*
- *How am I going to change it?*
- *What can I do on the next call to improve?*

After you have answered these questions, write down exactly what it is you have to do and say to improve. Then practice on the next call. This is a proven way to improve and make your improvement permanent.

Rule #3: Be Prepared For Objections

One of the biggest differences between the top 20% and the bottom 80% is that top producers are prepared in advance to handle objections. Let's face it, in sales you are going to get objections. The top 20% expect objections and are always prepared with scripted responses to handle them. Ask yourself:

- *What are the top three objections I get when I make cold calls?*
- *How about when I call a prospect back to close them?*
- *Am I prepared with scripted responses when I get these objections?*

When I say be prepared, I mean being ready for the selling situations, objections, brush offs, blow offs, put offs, and other types of sales resistance.

This book is packed with the precise skills, techniques,

strategies and scripted responses that help you handle most of the selling situations you find yourself in. It is up to you to learn them and use them. Prepare to win. Commit this week to developing and scripting responses to common objections. Here are some great resources for building scripts:

See your company's training material

Often times your company's sales training manual has valuable information for dealing with objections and common sales situations. Most of the time you only need to re-word and adapt them to fit your selling style. Your organization's proven training material is always the first place to start when preparing for objections.

Seek out your company's top closers

Perhaps the best way to hear how to handle common objections is to simply listen to the top closers in your company on the phone. Obviously, if they are top producers they're doing something right. You don't have to reinvent the wheel. Listen and write down what they say. Take them out to lunch and pick their brain. Model what they do and you will quickly find success.

Get a coach

It is your manager's job to provide you with all the tools you need to be successful, and in almost all cases they are ready and willing to help you. All you have to do is ask. If they can't help you directly, ask them where else you might go for the support you need. You may also choose to hire someone outside your organization to coach you. This is an excellent way to improve your skills. Coaches are helpful

> Practice doesn't make perfect. Practice makes permanent.

because they can see what you cannot see and will shine a light on habits and behaviors that are holding you back. To learn more about hiring and working with a personal coach go to *www.mrinsidesales.com/SecretResources.*

Read this book, and read it again

Use the scripts in this book to overcome the common objections you get. These scripts are proven and effective. I know they work because I use them every day to build my business. Once you have developed responses and scripts, commit to practicing and improving on every call. Practicing is the fastest way you will move into the top 20%. And here's the good news, you can begin doing that on your very next phone call.

> Your company's training material is always the first place to start when preparing for objections.

Rule #4: Know your numbers

The top 20% track and analyze their numbers. Knowing your numbers is critical to success. Here is a partial list of data you should be analyzing:

- *The best call times during your day.*
- *The number of phone calls you need to make before you get a qualified prospect.*
- *The number of prospects you have to call back before you close a sale.*
- *Your closing percentage.*
- *The number of leads you send out a day.*
- *The closing percentage on the leads you send out.*
- *The value of each golden hour.*

- *The value of each qualified prospect.*

I like to make three columns on a piece of paper - the first one for calls, the second one for contacts, and the third one for deals. I track how many phone calls I'm making every hour. This creates a sense of urgency. You will soon realize that even fifteen minutes off the phone can cost hundreds of dollars in lost income.

After I got to know my numbers I was much less likely to spend time chatting with people around the office, or wasting time in other ways. In fact, I began defending and protecting my right to be on the phone, and I became much more focused as a result.

When you begin tracking your numbers, you will have the data you need to set goals for improvement. Knowing where you are is the fastest way to get where you are going.

Rule #5: Record Yourself

How do you double your income in the next 90 days? Years ago, I was told that I could double my income in 90 days if I just recorded my calls and listened to them. It sounded too good to be true and frankly a little scary. But I was committed to improving so I tried it. The results changed everything for me.

The highest earning professionals are constantly analyzing their performance and making adjustments. To move into the top 20% you must do the same. The best way to do this as an inside sales professional is to record your calls and listen to both sides of the conversation. You will be amazed at what you hear when you listen to yourself.

The bottom 80% would never think about doing this, and if they did think about it, they wouldn't bother to follow through. Recording yourself will immediately separate you from that group. Here are some of the things to listen for while you review your recordings:

- *Did you give your prospect a chance to tell you everything?*
- *Did you talk over your prospect?*
- *Did you hear exactly what they were saying, or did you hear what you wanted to hear?*
- *Did you introduce an objection?*
- *Did you talk past the close?*
- *Did you ask the right questions based on what they said?*
- *Did you question the Red Flags?*
- *Did you even hear the Red Flags?*

I have to level with you. The first time you listen to yourself on tape will be very painful. I'll never forget the first time I heard myself on a call. It was terrible. I had to press stop several times because I couldn't stand the sound of it. I persevered, though, and after a while listening to my calls became easier. Soon I was making dramatic improvements.

One of the most exciting things about listening to your recordings is that you will learn more after just two or three recordings than in an entire year of sales training. Soon you will begin catching yourself using the right techniques and getting the desired results. You will begin catching yourself right before you begin speaking over your prospect, or introducing a new objection, or cutting someone off. And you will learn to listen to yourself and make adjustments.

> **How do you double your income in 90 days? Record yourself.**

If your company doesn't have a way to record your calls, go to *www.MrInsideSales.com/SecretResources* to find information on where to get a recorder. I guarantee that you will get more out of listening to your recordings than all the sales training courses and seminars in the world. By this time tomorrow you need to be recording yourself.

Rule #6 Listen

People ask me all the time if there is a single characteristic that defines a top 20% producer. I always tell them that the single greatest asset of the top 20% is their ability to listen.

Right now 80% of your competition is talking 80% of the time and barely listening the other 20%. They are more interested in pitching and trying to sell than listening for their prospects' needs and buying motives. On the other hand, the top 20% actually hear what their prospects say. They talk 20% of the time and listen the other 80%.

Listen to your recordings. How much of the time are you talking and how much of the time are you listening? You might be surprised. I remember when I began listening to my calls, I was amazed (actually appalled) by how bad I was. I loved to hear myself talk. I would go on and on. It took me months to actually learn how to listen. Here are five lessons I learned about listening:

Use a script

One of the biggest reasons sales reps don't listen is because they are too busy thinking about what to say next. This is especially dangerous during the qualification stage when your prospect is revealing why they will or won't buy. You *must* script your questions. By using a script, you will free yourself to really listen and pay full attention to what your prospect is saying.

Don't interrupt

I can't tell you how many times I hear sales reps interrupting their prospects while they are still talking. When you do this it is rude, disrespectful, and it demonstrates that you are not really listening. This is a very hard habit to break. But, by not interrupting you will often hear your prospect tell you exactly what you need to do to close them. If you have to, start using the mute button on your phone - you'll be amazed by what your prospects say . . . if you let them talk.

Pause

Allow some space after your prospect stops talking. Too many times salespeople think that just because the person on the other end of the phone pauses they are done talking. Not so. Most reps can't wait to start talking so they will jump in as soon as their prospect takes a breath. Develop the habit of pausing for a full 3 seconds after your prospect stops speaking — that's 1001, 1002, 1003. You will be amazed by how often they will fill the space and reveal crucial information that will help you close the sale.

> How much time are your talking? How much time are you listening? You might be surprised.

Keep them talking

If you haven't gathered the information you need to make the sale, use filler questions or openers like, *"Oh?" "Uh huh,"* and *"What do you mean?,"* to keep your prospect talking. Remember, they hold the key, and you will only get them to open the door if they are talking and you are listening.

Listen to your own recordings

Record yourself. Nothing will teach you how much you are listening (or not listening) than hearing yourself dealing with a prospect.

Rule #7 Pre-Call Planning and Scripting

One of the most effective habits you can develop is organizing your next day's work the night before. This way, as soon as you get into your office you are ready to hit the ground running, and you won't waste precious phone time.

- *Plan your closes.*
- *Review your prospects' buying motives and possible objections.*
- *Set a goal for the number of prospecting calls you will make.*
- *Organize your leads and call lists.*
- *Set three priorities.*
- *Group your non-essential activities and set aside time to complete them.*

You will save hours each week by being prepared for your day in advance. Just look around your office now and notice how much time 80% of your fellow workers waste each morning. Avoid this costly mistake and commit to preparing the night before.

Next, get your scripts together. It is crucial that you have scripts or at least specific outlines for exactly what you are going to say during each part of the sale. Here is a partial list of scripts you need to have ready before you pick up the phone:

- *Opening script*
- *Rebuttal/response scripts*
- *Qualifying checklist*
- *Closing script*
- *Closing rebuttal/response scripts*

The importance of scripts

Whenever the subject of scripts comes up, people usually have definite opinions. They either love them or hate them.

Those who wouldn't be caught dead using scripts like to point to those pesky telemarketers who call at night and sound stilted and computer like. *"I hang right up on them,"* they say. *"I'd never read a script. It's totally unprofessional."*

On the other hand, there are people (like me) who understand that some scripts, used in the right context, are exactly what separates the top 20% from the bottom 80% who are ad-libbing their way through calls.

The bottom line is that even if you are not physically reading a script, chances are you say the same things over and over again. And, chances are, if you haven't taken the time to plan out and script the absolute best, most effective, proven responses to the situations, objections, red flags, and reflex responses you get day in and day out, then you truly are winging it. And winging it is why so many salespeople crash and burn.

> Effective use of scripts separates the top 20% from the bottom 80%.

I'm big on scripts. To be successful you have to be prepared, you have to know what to say, how to say it, and you must know how to effectively deal with the objections and responses that blow off 80% of your competition.

Gatekeeper scripts

How successful are you at getting around gatekeepers? Do you cringe when you are asked, *"Will he know what this call is about?"* If you aren't using proven scripts to get past gatekeepers, then I know you are hating life. It doesn't have to be that way. I've included a whole section later on that deals with this completely, but here are a few pointers to get you started.   Use this, it works:

"Can I tell him who's calling?"

"Yes, please tell him Mike Brooks with Mr Inside Sales is holding please."

The combination of please -twice, and an instructional statement will eliminate 80% of any further screening.

Negative reflex response scripts

"I'm not interested."

"We do business with XYZ."

"We don't have the money now."

How do you feel when you hear these objections? These negative reflex responses usually mean the end for the bottom 80%. The top 20%, however, are prepared for these and have proven, scripted responses that work. Use this:

"That's exactly why I'm calling, you see..." (And then list a benefit your other clients are enjoying.)

This is just one proven and effective way to get past your prospect's negative reflex responses, and a way to earn the right to find out whether or not your prospect really is or isn't right for your product or service.

Voicemail scripts

Have you scripted an effective voicemail message that provides a benefit, creates curiosity, and gets your prospects to call you back? The worst thing you can do is *"um"* and *"uh"* your way through a voicemail message.

Rebuttal/ response scripts

80% of inside sales reps are ad-libbing and stumbling their way through easy rebuttals. Most of them are not getting deals done. You must script your rebuttals and responses.

I've included an entire chapter on how to handle the most common objections. However, before you go there, you must first learn how to find qualified buyers. That is the purpose of the next two chapters.

Real Secrets

- **The top 20% prepare to win.**

- **Become a sales professional.**

- **Practice doesn't make perfect, it makes permanent.**

- **Know your numbers.**

- **Record yourself.**

- **Learn to listen.**

- **Develop and use effective scripts.**

3 | *You Can't Close An Unqualified Prospect*

If I had to point to only one thing that differentiates the top 20% from the bottom 80%, it is their basic philosophy on generating and qualifying leads.

80% of companies and sales people are trying to generate leads to fill pipelines, while the top 20% are finding and qualifying real buyers.

There is a HUGE difference here. Most companies teach their sales reps to generate as many leads as possible, fill their pipelines, and then work these leads to get deals. As a result, there are thousands of salespeople creating, generating and stuffing their pipelines with non-qualified prospects who are never going to buy.

One of the key reasons 80% of sales reps fail is because they are pitching unqualified prospects. The top 20% understand this completely. Top producers are more interested in *disqualifying* prospects than in generating leads. This is one of the core reasons the top 20% have the highest closing ratios.

You can't close an unqualified prospect

Top 20% producers invest their time in finding and qualifying buyers (disqualifying the non-buyers). They don't waste time and energy on questionable prospects, and they aren't afraid to ask tough qualifying questions before engaging in the sales process. If a prospect is not qualified or does not have the ability to buy, they quickly move on.

Years ago I remember watching the top closer in my office hold his lead cards over his trash can while he qualified them. If he got two or three answers he didn't like, he would ask one more question, and if he still didn't get the answer he wanted, he would let the lead fall into the trash and move on. He used to say that prospects had to earn the right to make it onto his desk.

> Stop qualifying and start disqualifying your leads and prospects.

I was afraid to do this at first. But I learned hard lessons wasting hours with prospects who didn't buy. I changed my techniques and soon after, my results changed too. Suddenly, I understood why top 20% producers focus on disqualifying prospects.

Always remember that you don't need the practice of chasing and pitching unqualified leads; rather, you need the practice of pitching and closing qualified buyers. This chapter is designed to help you find qualified buyers. The scripts and techniques are proven - all you need is a commitment to use them on your next call.

Throw Your Sales Pipeline Away

Another name for the sales pipeline is the sales funnel. Imagine a funnel - big and wide at the top and small at the bottom. The idea is, if you put enough leads in the big end some deals will come out of the small end. Sales organizations and salespeople everywhere spend enormous amounts of time, energy, and emotion filling, managing, and analyzing the sales pipeline. They prospect and prospect, then hope and pray that deals come out the other end.

After they fill the pipeline they obsess over numbers and ratios, measuring what goes in and what comes out. Out of 10 leads they might close one deal, or out of 15 leads close one or two deals, and so on.

The problem with the pipeline concept is that salespeople become more focused on the number of leads and prospects they generate than with the quality of those prospects. The conventional thought process is, *"If we throw enough crap on the wall, some of it will stick."* Well, excuse the pun but that method stinks. And top producers know this.

The top 20% have thrown their pipeline away and instead they use a **sales cylinder** with a top end the same width as the bottom end. Top producers want as many leads to come out as they put in. So, unlike the bottom 80%, they spend most of their time *disqualifying* prospects and only allow in the select few who are highly qualified and likely to buy.

To create your sales cylinder first analyze the prospects currently in your pipeline and assign an "A" to the ones you know or are pretty sure will buy, a "B" to those that might buy (but you're not sure of), and a "C" to those you have no idea about or think won't buy. This step will not work unless you are brutally honest.

Next, to calibrate, track your closing ratios on each group (A's, B's, C's). Your closing ratio on A leads should be great, while most C leads will not close. Then begin system-atically and ruthlessly purging B and C prospects. Bottom line, stop spending time with unqualified leads and instead, find, qualify, and close real buyers.

Prospects Never Get Better

One of the best ways to determine who actually does make it into your *sales cylinder* is to pay close attention to the obvious red flags on your initial qualifying calls. In their haste (or desperation) to fill their pipeline, the bottom 80% overlook or ignore early red flags hoping that these disquali-fiers will miraculously go away once the prospect sees their information, product, or service. But, of course, they never do.

This is a crucial tenet of top 20% philosophy and you must understand it, believe it, and abide by it starting today. The fact is, deal killers on the front end will never go away. And the brutal reality is, leads and prospects never get better with time. You know in your gut this is true.

I can't tell you how many times I've sent information to prospects I knew were going to be trouble. Prospects who said they'd look it over but couldn't commit; or prospects who wouldn't give me the time to ask all my qualifying ques-tions, but rather rushed me off the phone; or prospects who told me they weren't in the market, but would always move on something if it was as good as I said it would be. I've spent long afternoons chasing unqualified prospects, and when I finally did catch them, I was sorry I had! None of them turned into deals.

You can't ignore these red flags! Do what the top 20% do: as soon as you hear something that triggers your intu-ition or that gives you that sick feeling in your gut, stop and ask a tough disqualifying question. Here are some examples you can begin using today:

If someone says that they usually buy from _____, but would like to see your information, ask:

"Why would you switch vendors?" or

"How many other companies have you looked at in the last six months?"

And then: "And how many did you go with?"

If someone says that they will pass your information on to _____, say:

"Thanks. So that I make sure I'm not wasting her time it's best that I speak with her for just a few minutes. Can you please tell her that (your name) is holding please?" If you're then told they are not available, make sure and get their direct line or that person's extension and keep calling until she picks up.

If someone says that they'd be glad to look it over, ask:

"Great, after you do, and if you think that it can help you (or your business, etc.), when would you move on it?"

Trust me, if you want to close like the top 20% then you have to start questioning the red flags. Remember, it is better to disqualify the non-buyers early than to spend your time and energy chasing and pitching people

> **The brutal reality is, leads and prospects never get better with time.**

who are never going to buy. Take a moment to script your own questions to the common red flags you encounter.

Reflex Responses

One of the most frustrating aspects of cold calling is getting blown off by a prospect's initial reflex objections. How many times have you heard, *"I'm not interested,"* or *"We're happy with who we have,"* when cold calling? These re-flex responses are why so many salespeople dread cold calling. What makes the top 20% so suc-cessful is that they are prepared for these reflex responses and easily get past them by using proven, scripted rebuttals. The good news is most reflex re-sponses fall into just four catego-ries:

> The top 20% are prepared to deal with reflex responses with proven scripts.

- *I'm not interested*
- *Just send information*
- *We're happy*
- *I'm too busy*

I'm not interested

This is the most common reflex response used to blow off and intimidate cold callers. Your goal here is simply to sidestep this common reflex response and get on with your pitch or questions. Here are three scripts to help you:

Script 1:
> *"That's fine and many of my best clients told me the same thing as well. But as they learned more about this and saw*

the benefits, they were glad they took a few minutes. One thing they liked…." (continue with your presentation)

Script 2:

"I didn't expect you to be interested, you don't know enough about it yet. But I do know you're interested in (provide a benefit here – saving $, increasing production, return, etc..)" (continue with your presentation)

Script 3:

"I can understand that _____. You probably get a lot of these kinds of calls. I know what that's like because I get a lot of calls, too. And once in a while I listen because every now and then something really good comes along. And that's what's happening for you right now. You see… (continue with your presentation)

Just send information

You are in the closing business, not the brochure business. Trial closes to assess their level of interest are what work best with this reflex response.

Script 1:

"I'd be happy to, and if you like what you see would you be ready to place an order?"

Script 2:

"Before I do, I want to make sure you'd be ready to act on it if you like it. Let me ask you … (qualifying questions on budget, decision-making process, etc.)"

Script 3:

"Sure, and after you review the information how soon are you going to make a decision?"

Script 4:
> *"And what would you need to see to say 'yes' to it?"*

Now you may be thinking, "Sometimes it takes five to seven *touches* before someone will buy, and sending information begins that process. How do I strike a balance or know when to just cut bait and not send anything?"

I understand it is important to build relationships and that sending information is part of a process, but that does not mean you shouldn't disqualify those who are just looking for an easy way to get you off the phone, or who are trying to blow you off. What you must do is ask questions like:

> *"I'd be happy to. What other kinds of information, companies, or solutions are you looking at now?"*

This tells you how many other people they have given this line to (and how many brochures they've collected and who your competition is), and then:

> *"And what do you like best so far?"*

This tells you about their decision process and, chances are, any objections or stalls they mention will be the same you will get when you call back.

> *"What has kept you from moving ahead with that?"*

Again, this will reveal their objections (as well as some of their buying motives). They may also come right out and say why they aren't buying anything right now. I'm sure you can think of some of your own questions, but the point is that before you just send your information, you've got to do your job and qualify.

We're happy

There are two possibilities when you hear this initial response. First, your prospect may be blowing you off. In this case your objective is to quickly get them interested and talking. Second, they may be happy now, *but things change.* Your goal is to get them to think of you when change occurs and to get information that will help you qualify or disqualify them for future calls.

Script 1:

> *"That's what a lot of my current customers said before they learned more about _____. Just out of curiosity what do you like most about your current (vendor, product, service)?" The key here is to get them talking.*

Script 2:

> *"That's excellent. Whenever you are getting a great product at a great price you should never think about switching. Out of curiosity, how did you make your decision to go with them?" Get them talking so that you can ask follow up questions that will help you further qualify the opportunity.*

Script 3:

> *"I'm glad you're taken care of right now. _____, let me ask you something. If you ever found it necessary to get another (quote, point of view, vendor, information, etc.), could I be the first one in line to talk to you about some of your needs? Great. I'll go ahead and send you some of my contact information; do me a favor and keep it with your (similar) records so you'll have it handy if you need some help with (your product or service)."*

After you have their information ask:

"Just out of curiosity _____ , what might have to happen for you to consider looking at someone different?"

I'm too busy

In the 21st Century when someone says they are too busy, they probably are. Pushing too hard against this reflex response will usually just cause stress for you and your prospect. The best thing to do is to set an appointment to call them back.

Script 1:

"That is exactly why I called. I know how busy you are and I wanted to set an appointment when both of us will have more time to talk. Would Thursday at 2:00pm work better for you?"

More than one objection

In conversations with prospects it is likely that you will get more than one objection. For example if someone says that they are *"too busy"* and you ask for another time to call, they will likely answer with another objection like, *"to tell you the truth I'm just not interested."* For this reason you must always be prepared for two no's or responses. Practice and practice until you don't have to think about what to say when you get the second reflex response. Begin using these scripts immediately to help you overcome the brush-offs that stop the bottom 80% in their tracks.

Getting Past the Gate Keeper

It is universal - salespeople hate gatekeepers! One of the main reasons is most don't know how to get past them.

Many reps resort to tricks that don't work and often make them look foolish. It is enough to make many good salespeople want to quit their jobs.

The top 20% don't play games. Instead they use straight forward proven techniques that work.

The top three techniques to eliminate screening:

- *Please use please*

- *Give your full name and company name*

- *Use instructional statements*

Please use please

The single most powerful technique to eliminate screening is to use please, please. Here's how you do it. Start your call with:

"Hi, could you please connect me with_____, please?"

Remember, it's a gatekeeper's job to SCREEN YOU OUT!

So when they ask:

"Can I tell him who's calling?"

You respond with:

"Yes, please, please tell him _____ _____ with the ABC Company is holding please." (Use please three times.)

ATTENTION: While this method seems overly simplistic in its approach, please don't underestimate its power! You will be amazed by its effectiveness.

Give your full name and company name

80% of your competition is trying to dodge or trick the gatekeeper. Perhaps the most overused trick is giving their first name as if they were a friend calling. Guess what happens? This only makes the receptionist mad, identifies you as a "pesky telemarketer", and it encourages more screening.

Don't play games. Always give both your name and your company name. You will sound more professional and your professionalism will be respected.

Use instructional statements

In addition to giving your name and company it is crucial to end with an instructional statement (remember, the primary function of a receptionist or secretary is to take instruction.) Examples of instructional statements:

Receptionist: "Can I tell him who's calling?"

"Yes, please, please tell him Mike Brooks with Mr Inside Sales is holding please."

Receptionist: "Can I tell him what this is about?"

"Yes, please tell him it's about our upcoming top 20% sales training, please. I'll hold while you put me through." or "While you get him."

Start now. Use these techniques on each cold or follow-up call. You'll be amazed by how many more decision makers you get through to and by your increased confidence.

The Qualified Prospect

So what exactly is a *qualified* prospect? Most sales-people and their managers won't be able to tell you. The reason is because they rarely take the time to define what qualified means for their product, service, or industry. Unfortunately, one of the key reasons the bottom 80% struggle to close business is their failure to fully qualify prospects.

> Do not spend time with prospects who are not fully qualified.

The top 20% do not spend time with non-qualified prospects. They do their homework up front and use a *Qualifying Checklist* as a guide. Before engaging in the sales process they ensure that each question is answered.

The six-step qualifying checklist:

1. *Why will your prospect buy?*
2. *Why won't they buy?*
3. *Who makes the decision?*
4. *What is involved in the decision process?*
5. *What/who is your competition?*
6. *What is the budget?*

Prospects should not make it into your sales cylinder until these questions have been answered. In fact, this may be a good time to answer these questions before moving forward with any of your current prospects. Here are specific questions to use with your qualifying checklist:

Why will your prospect buy? (buying motives)

- *What is this prospect looking for?*
- *What are their buying motivations?*
- *What do you need to say to get them to buy?*
- *What is important to them?*
- *Why did they buy last time?*
- *What would they like to change this time?*
- *If they could get what they wanted, what would that look like?*

   Sample Questions to reveal buying motives:

   "_____, what are you hoping to accomplish with this?"

   "What is most important to you when choosing a vendor/ company for this?"

   "If you could get everything you wanted from this (service/ product/solution), what would it include?"

   "Why did you buy the (service/product/solution) you did last time?"

   "What would it take for you to choose our company for this?" (My personal favorite!)

Why won't they buy? (potential objections)

- *Why are they getting another quote?*
- *What are some of their sore spots?*
- *What are they trying to avoid?*
- *Why didn't they buy last time?*
- *Why are they looking at different companies?*
- *Why have they waited this long?*

- *Why won't they buy?*

  Sample Questions to reveal potential objections:

  "Who do you usually get this (service/product/solution) from?

  "Are you going to get a quote from them as well?"

  "Why are you considering using a different (vendor/company/provider) this time?"

  "What other solutions are you looking at?"

  "I see you looked at our company before, what kept you from going with us?"

  "Sounds like you've had this problem/situation a while. What has kept you from doing something about it?"

Who is the Decision Maker?

- *Who is the decision maker?*
- *How many are there?*
- *Who do they consult with on this?*
- *How much influence do they have?*

  Sample Questions to find the decision maker:

  "_____, who will you be making this decision with?" (assumptive)

  "Besides yourself, who else will be weighing in on this decision?"

"_____, who has the final say on this?"

What is involved in the decision process?

- *What is the decision process like?*
- *What's involved?*
- *Who's involved?*
- *What happens next?*
- *How long does it take?*
- *How many other steps are involved?*

Sample Questions to uncover the decision process:

"_____, after we submit the (bid/proposal/send the information), what happens next?"

"How long does this process take?"

"Who's involved in that?"

"When would you like to see a decision made on this?"

Who is your competition?

- *How many other companies are they looking at?*
- *Is the company they're using now still involved?*
- *What are they looking for in their next vendor?*
- *How many other bids/quotes are they getting?*
- *Who do they like best so far?*
- *What would they like to improve upon?*

Sample Questions to discover your competition:

"Who else are you looking at for this?"

"What do you think so far?" (Great question!)

"Might you use the same company (providing the current service) again?"

"Who are you leaning towards so far?" (Crucially important – listen carefully!)

"Oh, why is that?"

What is the budget?

- *It's always about the money!*
- *What is their budget for this?*
- *What did they spend last time?*
- *How big of a position do they usually take?*
- *What is their limit?*
- *What would they feel comfortable spending?*
- *Is your product or solution within their budget?*
- *What's the most you could ask for?*

Sample Questions to uncover budget:

"What is your budget for this?"

"What did you spend last time for this?"

"If we could provide a solution you were comfortable with, could you afford $_____ amount today?"

"What is the ball park range you're looking to stay within on this?"

Are you getting a feeling for what a qualified prospect is? Pretty comprehensive isn't it? I think you would agree that the more information you get, the more qualified your prospects are going to be. And of course the more qualified a prospect is the higher the probability you will get the deal done.

Now I know what you may be thinking, "Mike, my prospects aren't going to just sit there and let me ask all those questions." You know what? You're right, many won't. But that is good news because this helps you separate the buyers from the non-buyers. Qualified buyers will always give you the time and respect you deserve. Certainly there will be times when your prospects are busy. In that event, schedule an appointment to call back when they are available to speak. I have created a qualifying checklist to help guide you. You can download it free at: *www.mrinsidesales.com/SecretResources.*

> Qualified prospects will always give you the time and respect you deserve.

Layering Questions

Once you have fully qualified your prospects, layering questions will help you uncover more information and get you closer to the close. Layering questions are designed to dig deeper into an area or concern so that you get to the root of what really drives your prospect.

A layering question:

"Who are you going to be speaking with about this decision?" (assumptive question)

And when they say their spouse, boss, or business partner, you then layer the question by asking:

"And what do they think you should do about this?"

Having this information gives you the edge when it is time to close. Layering questions are effective, powerful, and easy to execute. Yet 80% of sales reps never use them. The top 20%, on the other hand, know their value and ask them all the time.

More examples of layering questions:

"If you decide to move on this investment, how much would you put into it?"

Layering question: *"And is that money liquid now or would you have to move something around?"*

"I'll get this quote off to you today, and I'll follow up with you tomorrow at 10 o'clock – would that work?"

Layering question: *"Assuming you like it, what is the next step?"*

If your prospect says, "Go ahead and send your information and I'll review it."

Layering question: *"What are you specifically looking for in the information?"*

Layering questions draw out more information, and sometimes can be used to subtly call your prospect's bluff. Use your gut intuition to guide you. Take a moment to write down ten more layering questions specific to your selling situation.

Use Assumptive Questions

There are few questions more valuable than the assumptive question. While the bottom 80% use closed ended questions like, *"Are you the decision maker on this?,"* the top 20% effectively utilize the assumptive questions.

Consider this: most prospects you speak with will involve others in the decision-making process. But most of them won't tell you this until the end of your presentation.

Asking the closed-ended question, *"Are you the decision maker?"* often prompts them to say yes and you are stopped dead in your tracks. Using an assumptive question will often smoke this out. Here's what to say:

"_____, who else will you be speaking with in regards to this decision?"

When you ask an assumptive question like this, your prospect will often volunteer crucial information that will help you close the sale. This is information 80% of your competition is not getting.

More examples of assumptive questions

For budget: *"_____, most of my clients have a price range in mind when considering this, what is yours?"*

To sell bigger orders: *"_____, most of my clients want the discount that comes from ordering this by the (case, unit, multiple month contract, etc.), is that how you want to do this as well?"*

Assuming the close: *"_____, I've been looking forward to getting back with you today. I'm sure you've (reviewed the information, brochure, material, etc.) and liked what you saw. Did you want to start with (x size order) today, or take the (larger) order?"*

The assumptive questioning technique should be used throughout the sales process and will immediately make you a better closer. The main benefit of using assumptive questions is that they often catch your prospects off guard and eliminate the smoke screens they are so used to putting up.

Incoming Leads

The Internet has changed everything - especially how sales leads are generated. I get requests weekly from companies who want to know the best way to deal with incoming "warm" leads.

Most salespeople, managers, and companies make the false assumption that these leads are more qualified because they are calling or emailing in. This is the biggest mistake made with incoming leads.

Most salespeople mistake the implied interest of an inbound lead to mean these leads are qualified and ready to buy. Thinking that all they need to do to get the deal is explain their product or service, they immediately go into pitch mode rather than qualifying further.

The top 20%, on the other hand, know that warm leads can be among the biggest time wasters. So instead of pitching, they do what they always do, disqualify people who are *just looking* in order to find real buyers. They do this by asking qualifying questions.

> Fully qualify inbound leads before moving into the sales process.

Great qualifying questions for inbound leads

"Thank you for contacting us today. What was it about our ad/promotion/website that caused you to call us?" (listen for the buying motive)

"Who else are you looking into?" (listen for your competition)

"Who do you like best so far?"

"Why is that?"

"How long have you been thinking about (buying, investing, changing) something like this?" then,

"What has kept you from acting on this?" (listen for possible objections)

"When are you looking to make a decision on this?"

Qualify inbound leads as thoroughly as you would on any outbound prospecting call. To be a top 20% producer, you have to find qualified buyers, whatever the lead source.

A Great Qualifying Call

Not long ago, my neighbor put in a new driveway using beautiful paving stones that dramatically improved the look of his property. Comparing my old asphalt driveway, I quickly went over to one of the installers and asked for an estimate. *"You have to call our office,"* he explained as he gave me their business card. Later that day I called and left a message expressing interest in their paving stones. What happened next was one of the best sales calls I've heard in years.

A couple of days later, Brenda called and explained that she was returning my call about their driveways. The first thing she asked was how I heard of them. I told her my neighbor had used them to install a new driveway. She took down his complete address.

Next she asked me what I was interested in. I told her I wanted the same kind of paving stones my neighbor had installed (she listened very carefully and did not interrupt). I asked if she could send someone out to give me an estimate. She said she would be glad to do that, but first she needed to explain how they worked.

She began by telling me about the process and quality of their work. She said that first they removed the existing asphalt driveway and hauled everything away. Next they prepared the driveway by digging and leveling 12 inches deep and by pouring high-grade sand. They then packed it down so that it was as strong as concrete. Then they installed the paving stones and filled in the spaces with a premium finish sand. Brenda explained that my new driveway was guaranteed not to crack or fade for as long as I owned my home.

> Assumptive questions are among the most powerful questions in sales.

She then stopped and asked me if this was what I was looking for (great qualifying question). *I said 'yes'.*

She told me the cost of their minimum job was $6000, which would cover an area of approximately 600 square feet. She then asked if that was within my budget (a direct money qualifying question). *I said 'yes it was'.*

Brenda then asked if weekdays or weekends were best for my appointment. *I told her weekends.*

She offered two time slots for the following Saturday and asked, *"Is 10 AM good or is 1 PM better for you?"* I took the 10 AM spot. She said it was important that both my wife and I were there for the appointment and asked me if we both would be. *I said 'yes'.*

She confirmed all the details and gave me the name and cell phone number of the sales rep (closer) who would be out that next Saturday.

When I hung up the phone, I marveled at how the call had gone. I already felt closed! At this point the appointment with the sales rep felt like a formality. Brenda was clearly in the top 20%.

Is she missing out on some appointments by being so thorough? Probably. But is Brenda missing out on any real buyers? Probably not.

The lesson here is that by properly qualifying your prospects you can be sure you are only going to be spending time with those most likely to buy.

Leaving Effective Voice Mail Messages

I remember a time, not long ago, when voice mail was all the rage. There was no email, so people tended to honor and even return voice mail messages. Life was good.

But that's history. Email has changed everything, and people now hit the delete button on their voice mail messages the instant they hear something they don't like, which is usually when it's a message from an unknown sales rep. What to do?

One of the burning questions for 21st century sales professionals is, *"When should I leave a voice mail message?"* The answer: *it depends.*

If you are cold calling, it doesn't make sense to leave a voice mail message that has a very high probability of getting deleted. You will just waste valuable phone time plowing through their voice mail system leaving messages.

But if you are calling a prospect back, leave a message. If you are following up on an inbound lead, leave a message. If you are following up on a hot lead, leave a message.

The good news is there are proven techniques for leaving voice mail messages that get returned:

Be specific

It is imperative to do some research and leave a message that specifically addresses a problem or event that your prospect is dealing with. For example, if you find out on their website that they are opening a new branch or division in another city, mention this and tie it in with your value proposition. And, always use their first name. Something like:

> Poorly crafted voice mails are quickly deleted. Always use a voice mail script.

"Hi Barbara, Mike Brooks here with HMS software. I'm calling about your new office that's opening in Houston next month, and I wanted to provide you with some ideas that may help with your networking issues. We work with a lot of companies in the area, and I think you'll find it useful if we speak.

You can reach me by calling area code (818) 999-0869. That number again is area code (818) 999-0869, and ask for Mike Brooks. I look forward to speaking with you and thanks for returning my call."

Use a script

You absolutely must script out exactly what you are

going to say. Nothing gets your message deleted quicker than a series of *ums* and *uhs*. People are way too busy to sit through (let alone call back) a message that rambles on and on by someone who doesn't appear to know why they are calling. Also, by scripting your message you will create great content ahead of time and deliver it like a professional - unlike the other 80% of the messages they get.

State their problem and offer a solution

Did you notice that in the earlier voice mail example, I mentioned a specific event *(their new office)* and a possible problem *(networking issues)* as well as potential solutions to their problem *(some ideas that may help you)*?

This is the winning voice mail formula. Mention specific problems your prospect is having and offer your solutions to them. Prospects are only thinking about themselves and will only be interested in you if you can help them solve their problems. By addressing this in your voice mail, you stand the best possible chance of getting your call returned.

> People are way to busy too sit through a message that rambles on and on.

Describe how your solution has worked for others in their industry

Did you notice in the example voice mail message I said *"we work with a lot of other companies in your area"*? People want to work with, and in fact feel comfortable working with, people who understand their business. If you have experience solving another company's problems, then your prospect will want the same solution. Everyone wants to work with successful companies and if other companies are using you they figure you've got to be doing something right.

Never, ever leave more than two messages

After you leave your first message, wait at least a week before you leave a second. And if that doesn't get returned, move on. The last thing you want to be is a pest, and a desperate one at that. After two messages, your prospect has your name and number, and if they are interested they will call you back.

Using Email to Your Advantage

Email is the new voice mail – in fact, it's even better! Believe it or not, email is a great way to identify buyers because it has become the primary mode of communication with business people. Business people love email because they can see the message and respond at their own pace.

The five rules for effective email messages

1. Use the prospect's first name in the subject line.

2. Customize the message as much as possible: make it appeal to their needs (see voice mail rules above).

3. Keep it short! Break sentences into paragraphs to make them easy to read and more accessible. And, always proofread your message before clicking send.

4. Ask for a return response, whether they are interested or not.

5. Promise to follow up by phone if they don't respond.

Follow these rules and you will separate yourself from the bottom 80% and give your emails the best chance of being returned. Go to *www.mrinsidesales.com/SecretResources* for more information on sending effective email messages.

Overcoming Call Reluctance

Have you ever sat at your desk, shuffled your leads, looked at the clock thinking that lunchtime was way too far off, and then prayed for the phone lines to go dead? Has the phone ever seemed like a 200-pound weight? If so, then you know what call reluctance is. Before I became a top 20% producer, I had these feelings all the time. I hated Mondays, hated my job, hated rejection, and dreaded making calls. My paycheck was evidence.

One of the biggest reasons people experience call reluctance is because they are afraid people are going to say no. In other words, they fear rejection. People ask me all the time, *"How do I deal with the constant no's?"* My answer is simple - *I expect them.*

Most of the people you speak to will never buy. Most of the people you speak with are not going to be interested. That is just the way it is in sales and it is something you must come to grips with.

Instead of becoming frustrated with rejection, the top 20% embrace it. Their mind set is that the quicker they can move past the non-buyers, the faster they will uncover the buyers. When I'm cold calling, I expect most people will say no, so most of the time I get what I already expect. I'm not upset when people tell me no. I actually thank them for revealing themselves as non-buyers. And I smile because I know it just means that I will not waste valuable time on someone who is not going to buy, and I'm that much closer to a deal.

Of course the fastest way to overcome call reluctance is to make a real commitment to become a top 20% producer. When you do you will find that you overcome your fear because you become focused on your future rather than your fear. Here are five ways to overcome call reluctance:

Get excited

How much money could you earn if you were in the top 20% in your sales organization? Think about it. That is something to get excited about. Think about your goals, the things you want, the places you want to go, the peace of mind, and the respect you will receive when you are on top of the sales ranking list.

Commit

Make a commitment TODAY to do whatever it takes to become a top 20% producer. Your mantra should be, "If they (the top 20%) can do it, I can do it better!" It all starts with a decision and a commitment.

Invest in yourself

Learn and practice the skills, techniques and strategies of top 20% closers. Become a student of your craft. Read books, listen to audio programs and podcasts, attend seminars, and get a coach.

Harness your desire

How much do the top 20% in your company/industry make? How will your life change once you become one? What are some of the direct benefits you will enjoy? What kind of car will you drive? How will it feel to be debt free? Where will you live? What is it you really want? Identify how it will feel every day to wake up and know that you have achieved your goals. Get crystal clear.

> The #1 cause of call reluctance is fear.

Act as if

Change your self-talk. Affirm daily that you are already in the top 20%. Once you create this reality on the inside, your outside will change to reflect your new *inner reality.*

I guarantee that if you follow these five steps, your whole life will change. On Monday mornings, you will be the first one in the office and you won't be able to get on the phone fast enough. Your call reluctance will turn into call urgency. I know because it happened to me.

Real Secrets

- The bottom 80% focus on filling their pipe-line. The top 20% find buyers.

- Bad prospects never get better.

- Be prepared for reflex responses.

- Use please, please to eliminate call screening.

- Use the Qualifying Checklist to uncover real buyers.

- Don't spend time with prospects who are not going to buy.

- Use layering questions to dig deep into buying motives.

- Use assumptive questions to get past smoke screens.

- Use voice mail and email effectively.

4 | *Getting To Closed*

The number one question asked by salespeople and sales managers is, *"How do I close more sales?"*

My answer: You close more sales by spending time with more qualified prospects.

Most salespeople hate to hear my answer because they are not willing to put in the time and energy to thoroughly qualify and disqualify leads. They want it easy. So they fill their pipelines with unqualified prospects and hope for the best.

Here's the real deal

The close is set up by the qualification call. If you have followed the advice in the previous chapter (filled out your qualifying checklist, questioned the red flags, identified the buying motives, etc.) then you are ready to begin closing sales like the top 20%. Closing qualified leads is fun and easy to do. It is what the top 20% live for. The techniques in this chapter are designed to help you work with, and close, qualified prospects.

Listen Like a Detective

I once watched a news interview with a police detective. The detective was discussing various interrogation techniques, and he said something that I thought was brilliant and completely applies to sales.

The detective said that when you ask a question you should never say or do anything that might cause your suspect (prospect) to stop talking. In other words, you listen. You listen with full attention, and you do not interrupt with more questions. You just keep listening even when you think they are done talking. In sales, and especially inside sales where you don't have visual cues, listening is the most important single skill to develop. Here are five techniques to improve your listening:

> One of the biggest reasons salespeople fail to listen is they are too busy thinking about what to say next.

Use a script

One of the biggest reasons sales reps don't listen is they are too busy thinking about what they are going to say next. This is especially dangerous during the qualification stage when your prospect is revealing why they will and why they won't buy. This is why you must script your questions! By using a script, you'll be able to really listen and pay full attention to what your prospect is saying.

Don't interrupt

I can't tell you how many times I hear sales reps interrupting and talking over their prospects. Not only is this rude and disrespectful, but it demonstrates to their prospect that they are not really listening.

Early in my career, in order to learn how to listen I

had to literally put my hand over the mouthpiece and hold it above my head! By not interrupting though, I often heard my prospect tell me exactly what I needed to do or say to close the deal.

Get in the habit of catching yourself interrupting your prospects and start using the mute button on your phone. You will be amazed by what they are trying to tell you!

Pause

Always pause and take a breath after you think your prospect is done talking. Many sales reps can't wait to start talking so they will jump in as soon as their prospect takes a breath. A good habit to get into is to pause a full three seconds after you think your prospect is done speaking—that's 1001, 1002, 1003, before you say anything. You will be amazed by how often your prospect fills the space and reveals crucial information that helps you make the sale.

Use "Oh?", "Uh huh," and "What do you mean?"

If you have not uncovered the information you need to make the sale, use one of the above techniques to keep your prospect talking. Remember, they hold the key as to why they will (or won't) buy, and you will learn this only if they are talking and you are listening.

Listen to your own recordings

Recording yourself is the best way to learn when you are not listening. Nothing brings this home more than hearing yourself talk over people, interrupt, or just plain miss what they are saying. If you are not recording yourself, invest in a recorder. It will be one of the best investments you ever make.

These are simple yet powerful ways to improve as a listener. Just remember, above all don't do or say anything that might cause your prospect to stop talking. Keep listening.

Build Rapport

Building rapport is a core part of the selling process because people buy from people they like, know, and trust. Of course many people think it is difficult to build rapport over the phone. Actually, it is very easy. Use these three techniques to build rapport and get the person on the other end of the phone to like, know, and trust you.

Listen and acknowledge

Nothing kills rapport faster than if your prospect feels like you are not hearing what they are saying. To avoid this, pause briefly after they are done talking and before you begin speaking, and acknowledge what they just said. This can be accomplished with a simple, *"Oh, I understand,"* or *"I know what you mean,"* or even repeating or restating a portion of what they just said.

Use self-disclosure

When listening, find ways to identify with what your prospect is saying. Then, share a little bit of your experience by saying something like, *"I know what you mean. I do the same thing,"* or *"That's happened to me, too."* This is a great technique, but be careful. You don't want to disclose too much; this is, after all, a business transaction and your objective is to gain a new client, not a new best friend.

Use empathy

This is especially important when dealing with an angry or upset client. If something has gone wrong, resist the temptation to defend. Instead, acknowledge their feelings:

"That must be so frustrating to wait a week for your order and then have it arrive incorrect. I'm so sorry that happened." or,

"I had something like this happen to me, too, and I know how frustrated you must be."

People want to be heard, they want their feelings acknowledged, and to know that someone cares. Using empathy in these situations not only calms them down, but helps build rapport as well. In the end, people do prefer to buy from people they like, know and trust. Building rapport over the phone is as simple as listening, acknowledging, finding common ground, and being polite and empathetic.

> Use the qualifying checklist to prepare for the close.

Prepare To Close

At this stage in the game you should have collected a great deal of information on your qualifying checklist (get a free copy at *www.mrinsidesales.com/SecretResources*). To prepare for the close begin by reviewing this valuable information carefully. Make sure you are clear on your prospect's unique buying motives and be prepared to build a bridge from your product or service to those motives.

Find the buying motive

Recently a sales professional I was coaching shared this situation with me: She was asking for the order from a prospect when he announced that he had done some research and found that a competitor had a lower price for the same service. Sound familiar?

He said that if she could match the price then he would go with her company. She told me the problem was that she couldn't match the price. What should she have done, she asked? My answer: *"Find his real buying motive."* I told her I would have asked the prospect the following question:

> "_____, *I'm not saying I can match this price, but if I can, and with all things being equal, why would you go with me and my company and not the other?"*

This single question would reveal why he preferred her company, and that buying motive would become the leverage she needed to close the sale right then.

In the end, even though she couldn't match the price, she told me that the prospect called her back and purchased the service from her. I asked why and she said the prospect explained that he liked the way she dealt with him, took time with him, and explained things thoroughly.

This was his real buying motive (doing business with someone he trusted), and it outweighed the difference in price. Had she asked the question suggested earlier she probably would have been able to close the sale on the spot. Understanding your prospect's real buying motive is often the difference between making the sale or not. Sometimes all you need to do is ask a simple question to find that out.

> You must understand your prospect's real buying motive.

Deal with initial resistance

Even when you are working with qualified leads, you will still encounter initial resistance. *"I'm not interested,"* or *"I don't have time,"* are two of the most common brush-offs prospects use.

Let's face it, your prospects are getting a lot of calls, and they are not going to take time to listen to every salesperson who comes along. To deal with this, they have developed habitual reflex objections. It doesn't mean they won't or don't want to buy. These objections are just habits and come out automatically.

The top 20% know this in advance and are prepared for this resistance with proven, scripted responses that work. Here are some ways to handle initial resistance:

Initial resistance

"I looked it over and I'm/we're not interested."

Response:
"I understand, and that's perfectly OK. At first many of our clients don't fully understand the benefits of this and that's why I'm here. But let's do this. I'll take a few minutes to explain how this might help you, and if after you understand it you still think it's not for you, we'll part friends. Do you have that information handy?"

Response:
"I didn't expect you to be interested! Heck, if this thing sold itself, they wouldn't need me – they'd just send out the information and clients would send in checks! But seriously, this (product/service/investment) has many features that my clients now enjoy and can't live without, and it may be that way for you, too. Do yourself a favor and spend a few minutes with me to find out how and if this would be right for you. Go ahead and grab the information/quote/brochure and let me cover a few things – do you have it handy?"

Response:
"I understand, and some of my best clients said that at the beginning as well. But I'm sure you'd agree that any decision you make, whether it's a yes or a no – and believe me I can take either one – is best made once you understand all the facts, right? Well, I'm here to help you learn those, so grab that information, let's go over it, and if at the end it's not for you we'll part friends. Do you have it handy?"

Initial resistance

"I don't have the time right now."

Response:
"I know that feeling, my schedule is pretty full as well. Should I call you back in an hour, or would later this afternoon be better?" (Then make a definite appointment to call back.)

Initial resistance

"We don't have the budget/money right now."

Response:
"I completely understand and the first thing we need to do is find out whether or not this solution is even a good fit for you (or your company). Let's put the money aside for a moment and talk about this product/quote/service. Do you have that handy?"

Response:
"I can understand that _____. At first many of my clients felt they couldn't find the budget for this but after we went over how much they could actually save by using this product/service, they were glad they took a few minutes to

go over how this works. I think you will be happy as well. Do yourself a favor and grab that information – I'll hold on while you do."

The secret to handling initial resistance is not trying to overcome it. By doing that you're only feeding into it. Your goal when handling initial resistance is to *sidestep* it and get into your presentation.

Avoid the Biggest Mistake in Closing

It sends chills down my spine. In every company I work with, I hear 80% of sales reps begin their closing calls with the statement: *"I'm just calling to follow up…"* To be a top 20% closer it is absolutely critical that you understand that you are not calling to:

"Follow up," or

"See if they got the information," or

"See if they had time to go over it," or

"To find out if they have time to go through it."

You are calling back to take control of the close and to get the prospect to buy. The way the top 20% do this is by being prepared with scripted openings that work.

Sample opening

"Hi, _____, this is Mike Brooks calling with Mr Inside Sales. I've been looking forward to speaking with you, and I'm sure you've looked at the information I sent and probably

even have a few questions. Do me a favor and grab that, and I'll hold on while you do."

This works because it is assumptive, you are in control, and it overrides any initial resistance.

Sample opening

"Hi _____, this is _____ _____ with the ABC company, how are you doing today? Great. _____, it's been an exciting morning here, and I've got some updates I think you'll be interested in regarding that (quote/brochure/ information/demo) I sent to you. It'll just take a minute to bring you up to speed, so do me a favor, grab that (quote/ brochure/information/demo), and I'll be happy to hold on while you do."

Sample opening

"Hi is that _____? Hi _____, this is _____ _____ with the ABC company, how have you been? Gee I know the feeling. _____, the good news is that this won't take long, and you'll be glad you took a few minutes to go over this briefly. Do you have the (quote/brochure/information/ demo) handy, or should I hold while you grab it?"

The key to moving to the close is to be assumptive, assumptive, assumptive!

Bonus: The Instant Close

Before moving forward I want to teach you a short-cut that may instantly close the deal. While 80% of your competition believe they have to go through a lengthy presentation before asking for the sale, the top 20% know a much better way.

They use a powerful technique that gets the deal done without any objections and in 1/10 the time others usually take. It's easy! All you have to do is *ask for the sale in the beginning.* When you do the proper qualifying job on the front end, you will be surprised by how easy and successful this technique can be. And it's loaded with benefits:

Be:
Assumptive!
Assumptive!
Assumptive!

- First, some prospects are ready to buy but just have a couple of questions.

- Some have decided to buy and will appreciate that they won't have to sit through a long presentation.

- Others will have some concerns, but are essentially on board. Getting to their concerns up front makes everything easier.

- Asking for the deal right away also exposes who is NOT going to be a deal and saves valuable time going through a lengthy presentation.

- Others will give you some concerns and thus a good idea of how much work – and what direction – you need to take to close them.

Sample instant close script

"Hi _____, this is _____ _____ with the ABC company, how's your day? Well, I must tell you that I've been looking forward to speaking with you today. You see, I was thinking

about how happy my other clients are, and how much I enjoy talking to them, and I realized that you could easily become one of my best clients as well.

Now I'm sure you've reviewed the (quote/brochure/ information/demo), and, like them, you probably see the benefits it can bring to you. My question is, would you like to start with the (larger order here), or take our starter position of just (medium size order here)?" Shut up and listen.

Sample instant close script

"Hi _____, _____ here with ABC, how have you been? Great, you know I just got off the phone with one of my best clients, and he reminded me why I love my job.

You see, I get to work with people like you, I get to help you get the (benefits of your product) you need, and then I get an ongoing relationship that grows over time. And it all starts today!

Now I'm sure you looked over the (your product), and I'm sure you see how it can help you. My question is simple: would you like to get started with the quote as it is, or would you like to double up on that amount and save an additional 10%? You tell me." Shut up and listen.

Script Your Presentation

The top 20% plan and script their presentations. Not every word, they would have to give their prospect a script, too, if they scripted every word. The bottom line is that they say the same things, in the same way, over and over again.

The bottom 80%? They are often just making it up as they go along. And they sound like it, too. Nothing turns a prospect off more than having someone ad lib their way through an unorganized sales presentation. *"Oh, but I'll sound like a telemarketer!"* If that's going through your head right now, then maybe you already are one. The top 20% use (*but don't sound like they use*) a script. And there are many reasons why they are using one. Here is why the top 20% use a script:

> **The bottom line is scripts equal success!**

You sound professional

I don't know about you, but when telemarketers call me and begin saying, *"Um, I was ah calling for, um…"* I hang up immediately. Remember, your prospect can't see you, they only have your voice. When you follow a script you can actually concentrate on the delivery of your presentation, concentrating on the pace, the pitch, the timing, etc.

Most importantly, you sound confident. And people want to buy from people who are confident and believe in their product. Using a carefully crafted script will automatically build this confidence.

You remain in control

By using a script you know where you are, where you're going and, when you get questions, you won't get sidetracked.

You concentrate on listening

Because you are not thinking about what to say next you will actually pay attention to your prospect: how they breathe, the tone of their voice, how they ask questions, and the substance of their questions.

You won't introduce objections

This is a common, horrible mistake in sales. Anyone who has been in sales for any length of time has done it. By following a script, you will be forced to say the right things, close when appropriate, and keep asking for the order after answering an objection, rather than introducing more of them.

You won't talk past the close

When you use a script, you are forced to ask for the order because there is an actual end to your presentation. Using a script opens the door to effective presentations.

Start today by developing your own script. Look at your company's current scripts, or talk to the top 20% in your company and write down what works for them. Speak with your manager or company owner and have them develop one (*or close them on hiring me to write them for your company*). Whatever you do, get a script, presentation format or outline, and use it.

The Power of Trial Closes

One of the reasons many people find selling over the phone challenging is because there are no visual cues to tell them how their prospect is reacting to the presentation. Are they bored? Ready to buy? Did they understand what you just said? Are they with you? 80% of salespeople can't answer any of these questions, but top 20% producers can. That is because the top 20% use trial closes, while qualifying and closing to get this crucial information. Trial closes can be:

Subtle pulse takers

"Are you with me on that?"

"Does that make sense?"

Targeted

"Is that what you are looking for?"

"Is that going to fit your situation?"

"Is that within your budget?"

"Can you see the benefit here?"

Direct closing questions

"If this was all you knew about this, would you be tempted to buy it/go with it/hire us?"

"Does this sound like the solution you need?"

"Am I getting close to having a new client?"

Trial closes are an excellent way to take your prospect's pulse, and to find out how close you are to the sale. As a top 20% closer, you want to know this information and if you get a response that isn't getting you closer to a sale, stop and deal with it! Otherwise it will just come up at the end (after you've wasted time delivering your presentation) when you ask for the order.

> The top 20% use trial closes to check their prospect's pulse.

The Take Away Close

The most powerful close in sales and life is the take away. The reason it works is because *we all want what we can't have.*

You experience this all the time. Ever been to a restaurant and tried to decide between several items? As soon as the waitress tells you the X choice is sold out, what do you want?

Try it with your kids. Give them three options, two of which you know they want and one that is only so/so, then take that one away. Guess which one they will cry over?

It is the same in sales. I was once coaching a client and he was telling me about an objection he kept getting. After I gave him a response for it he asked, *"What happens if they still object?"* I answered *"Take it away."* By taking it away he would either build interest (and call his prospect's bluff) or get a non-buyer off the phone. Either way, he wins and leaves feeling in control and confident (that's the second greatest feeling next to getting a deal) - it is a top 20% feeling. Here are some examples of the take away:

> The most powerful close in sales is the take away.

This isn't for everybody

"_____, this product/service isn't for everybody. The companies/people who do use/buy/order/invest in it already understand the benefits and wouldn't use anything else. If you don't understand them now, you probably will later. If there are any available later on, I'll be happy to offer them to you but they are selling out quickly at this price. Do you want to take that risk?"

Others are waiting

"_____, it doesn't matter to me if you take this now, because I've got 10 other clients waiting for my call. They already understand the value here and will close this out whether you do it or not. It's for your benefit not mine that I'm offering this. You tell me, do you want to make a great decision now or should I just give your spot to someone else?"

Supplies are short

"_____, there are only X cases of this left and it doesn't matter to me if you buy them now or if my next client buys them. Somebody will in the next hour or so. If you'd like to wait that's your decision. Should I just call _____ and offer it to them?"

If you don't see the value

"_____, either you get the value of this or you don't -- it doesn't matter to me. I'd be happy to call you back in six months, and if we have this product/price/special available then as well you can act on it. I doubt we will but it is up to you. Do you want to move ahead with this now or should I just offer this to (their competitor)?"

The important thing is not to worry if they don't buy - some people won't! Just don't beg a deal, ever, instead use these takeaways and stay strong.

The Multiple-choice Close

A very effective close is the multiple choice close. A mistake many salespeople make is asking for the minimum order and being happy and satisfied when they get it. Because you never know how much a prospect or company can handle, you should stop robbing yourself of thousands of potential dollars by selling yourself short. By using the multiple-choice close you can avoid this. It goes like this:

> "_____ some of our clients start with the minimum (investment, package, order) of $5,000 and usually wish they had taken more, while other clients realize that with an (investment, product, service) this good it makes sense to move other things around to get more liquid (free up the budget) and participate at the $25,000 to $50,000 level. And, of course, our professional clients won't even consider anything less than $100,000 in something this good. Where do you see yourself starting?"

Now sit back and let your prospects sell themselves. You will often be surprised by how much larger of an order you will get. This one technique alone can double your income selling over the phone.

The Drop Close

If your prospect is interested in your product or service, but can't afford to buy the top model, or all the extras, or even participate at the minimum level of units, you can still get the sale by using the drop close. Although this is one of the best ways to save a sale, it is also one of the most abused closes. That's because weaker closers use it too soon.

The drop close, as the name suggests, is when you drop the minimum, or cut the price (if possible) of your product or service.

It should only be used after you are sure that your prospect wants to purchase or participate in your product or service and should then only be used with the words, *"I'm not saying I can, but if I could get you (a lower price or amount), can you move on this today?"* Here is how it works:

> *"I can understand that your budget may be a little tight right now, but I also know that you really would like to participate in this program (take advantage of this offer, use us for this service, etc) right? Well _____, sometimes a split position (minimum size, etc.) does become available and if it is not already spoken for, and if my manager approves it, I can sometimes offer it to new clients like yourself.* **Now I'm not saying I can, but if I could** *get you a starting position today at just half the price of the regular unit, is that something you would move on right now?"*

Now listen carefully to what they say. If they agree to move, put your prospect on hold and then come back and close the sale.

The Building Value Close

Sales professionals around the world are admonished daily to build value when their price is higher than the competition. They are instructed to stress the quality, the warranty, the features, etc. Unfortunately, 21st century prospects have heard it all before.

However, the fact remains that prospects most often buy from people they like, know, or trust. Your enthusiasm for your product or service is a big factor in getting your

> Use your enthusiasm to build value for your product or service.

prospects to like and trust you. I use the following script to not only build value in my product or service, but also to build value in myself. If your prospect says, *"I can get it cheaper,"* or *"Well the XYZ company has something similar for less money,"* or anything like that, here's what to say:

"You know _____ , I'm aware of all the other options for this (product or service) and quite frankly if I thought any of them were better for my clients, I'd be working there and selling them."

"When I got into this industry I did my own research, and I looked for the best company that not only offered the best (product or service) but also delivered the best customer service and follow-up. I chose (your company) because they give my clients the best overall value and the best experience, and that means they continue to do business with me and refer new business to me as well."

"If there was a better product or company for you to be doing business with I'd be there and we'd be talking about that. But there isn't."

"Bottom line, if you want the best overall value, results and experience with this (your product or service) then do what I did - choose (your company). You'll always be glad you did. Now, do you want to start with the X size order or would the Y size order be better?"

This technique builds value in the most important part of any sales transaction - you! Use it each time you get the price/competition objection and watch your sales and confidence grow.

How to Handle the Price Question

It is important to understand that a question about price is not the same as a price objection. Many salespeople are taught to deflect price questions or are afraid to be straight with their prospect. The top 20% don't see it this way because they understand that the most important part of the price question is not the answer to the question but instead what happens next. Here is a multiple choice question:

After giving your prospect the price should you:

A) Remain silent, waiting for them to ask another question
B) Keep pitching their product or service
C) Move on to another qualifying question
D) None of the above

The answer: *D) None of the above.* If you do A, B, or C you are missing the opportunity to find out where your prospect stands in regards to budget.

The right approach is to ask them how they feel or where they stand relative to the price you just gave them. Use any of these:

"How does that price sound to you?"

"Is that within your budget?"

"Which of those price points appeal to you the most?"

"Is that what you are looking to spend?"

Whenever your prospect asks about the price, and you give it, you must qualify their budget. The top 20% automatically do so and move that much closer to getting the information they need to close the sale.

The bottom 80% miss this golden opportunity because they are afraid to ask tough qualifying questions. Use these price qualifying questions every time you are asked about the price - the information you get will move you closer to closed.

Prospects Who Are Avoiding You

Even with the best qualifying skills, some prospects will not be interested or will have made another decision. That's OK. Not everybody is going to buy. The key to successfully dealing with these prospects is to make sure you stay in control and disqualify them early on in the sales cycle so you don't waste your time or energy.

You will know you are dealing with this kind of prospect because suddenly they are hard to reach, don't return calls, or give vague answers. Realize that if your prospect isn't calling you back or the answers to your questions are vague, or noncommittal, then it is probably time to move on. The problem for the bottom 80% is that they will chase and chase these prospects because it seems easier than cold calling and looking for real buyers.

Learn to move on!

"At least they took the information or have a need," they say. But are they buying? Usually not. And all that wasted energy and time just puts them further behind. The solution? Ask tough questions! In other words, when you do get your

hard-to-reach prospect on the phone, ask them point-blank where they stand. Try this:

"_____ , *let me ask you a question and please be honest. We've talked about this now for X amount of time (or you've had this information for X amount of time), and I don't want to keep bothering you if this isn't a fit. So let me ask you: Does this look like a solution you'd actually take action on, or do you have something else in mind?*"

Call them out. Non-buyers will quickly go away, while qualified prospects will tell you what is really going on.

Get Your Prospect Involved

The top 20% establish and maintain control of the close. They do this by getting their prospect involved - especially at the beginning. This helps them gauge their prospect's level of interest, and decide when it is time to take the prospect all the way through the close. These techniques will help you involve your prospect:

- During the qualifying call ask your prospect to *"Grab a pen and a piece of paper,"* and have them write down things like a benefit, the price, your name, your company name and phone number, your next appointment time, etc.

- At the start of the close, have them physically get the information, the quote, material, demo, etc., and never begin your presentation until they do.

- During your presentation, have them get their calculator out and crunch the numbers with you or have them write out specific details about your product or service.

Any way you can get your prospect involved helps you gain control and also commits them more to you and to your product. Obviously the less the prospect cooperates the lower their interest. This is what is so great about this technique. It tells you who's real and who's not, and how much work you have left to do.

Taking Your Prospect All the Way

This is a subtle but important technique. It is assumptive in nature, directive in its execution, and allows closers to keep both momentum and control all the way to the end. While most salespeople have been taught to ask for the deal (and some actually do), most finish with something like:

"So how does that sound?"

"Have I answered all your questions?"

"Would you like to place the order now?"

"So let's get you started..."

The problem with all these closing attempts is they are weak. The sales rep is hoping that by some miracle the prospect will close themselves. The top 20%, on the other hand, don't ask for the deal, rather, they assume it and take the prospect all the way through the close. Here's how they do it:

"Great _____, so let's get you started with this. You are going to need a pen and that purchase agreement I sent you. It's the document at the back in green, do you see that? Great, now go ahead and start by filling out…"

See the difference? The top 20% know they are dealing with a qualified prospect because they qualified them by asking tough questions, presented solutions, and used trial closes. The top 20% know where they stand. Because of this, they know when it is time for the prospect to buy.

But they don't leave this very important decision up to the prospect. Rather, they keep control of the call, assume the deal, and take their prospect all the way. The top 20% believe that after they have done all this work, they deserve to get the deal and that the prospect expects to buy.

This is a powerful top 20% closing secret, and you can increase your closing ratio by 50% or more by using it. Try it this week and watch your sales soar!

Real Secrets

- **The secret to closing more deals is working with more qualified prospects.**

- **The top 20% are prepared to close before they pick up the phone.**

- **The instant close technique is a powerful tool in the top 20% tool box.**

- **Script your presentations.**

- **Use trial closes to constantly gauge your prospect's interest.**

- **The take away is the most powerful closing technique.**

- **Your enthusiasm for your product or service and your rapport building skills are the greatest builders of value.**

- **Use price questions to qualify budget.**

- **The top 20% take their prospects all the way.**

5 | *The Objection*

As you can imagine, sales reps hate getting objections because their hearts sink into their stomachs, their palms start to sweat, and they have to scramble for answers. For this reason, most salespeople are convinced that learning how to overcome objections is the real secret to closing more deals. However, the real key to closing sales is spending more time with more qualified prospects. Of course, that does not mean that you won't get objections, just that how you deal with them will be different.

When sales reps ask me how they should handle objections, they are often surprised by my reply. I tell them they should never answer objections.

They look at me like I'm crazy. I explain that most objections are just stalls or smokescreens hiding other objections that your prospect doesn't want to disclose. As soon as you begin answering objections, have you ever found that they just have another and yet another?

So here's what you do: instead of answering an objection you first isolate and question it. Let's look at two of the most common objections to illustrate what I mean.

> *If the prospect says, "Your price is too high," respond with:*
>
> *"I can understand that, and let me ask you a question -- if this price was exactly what you were willing to pay, is this (your product/service, etc.) the solution you would go with today?" Shut up and listen.*

Now that you have isolated the objection you will find out if price really is the only objection. If you get any answer other than *yes* then price isn't what is stopping your prospect from moving forward. This means you have more work to do to find the real roadblock.

> *If the prospect says, "I've got to speak to, talk this over with . . .," respond with:*
>
> *"I can totally understand that _____, and let me ask you - if you did speak with _____ and they said whatever you thought was fine with them, would you go with this today?"*

Again, any answer other than *yes* and this objection is just a stall. Answering it will get you nowhere. Do you see how this works? The whole point of isolating and questioning the

> **Don't answer objections. Isolate and question them.**

objection first is to uncover what is *really* holding your prospect back. Until you find that out, you are a long way from a deal. So stop answering objections and start isolating them. You will become a much stronger closer.

The Five-Step Method for Objections

While isolating and questioning objections is the most important step for handling them, it is just part of a process. The Five-Step Method is how the top 20% deal with objections. Here's how it works:

Step 1 - use a softening statement

Hear your prospect out completely and use a softening statement.

"I completely understand how you feel."

"Some of my best clients felt that way also."

Example:
"I completely understand how you feel, this is a big decision, and right now I'm sure it makes sense for you to think about this."

Step 2 - isolate and question the objection

Isolate and question to ensure that you are dealing with the real objection.

Example: *"The price is too high."*

"I understand _____, and let me ask you a question: Assuming that the price on (your product or service) weren't an issue (or fit within your budget, or if someone were suddenly going to buy them for you), but if price weren't an issue here, is this the solution you feel is right for you today?" Or, *"Is this something you would go ahead and order today?"*

Step 3 - answer the objection

Once you have uncovered the real objection, use a scripted response to answer the objection. No secret here that I'm recommending you use a scripted response. Either use one of the scripts you already have, or use one of the scripts in the next section and adapt it to fit your product or service. No matter what though, use a script.

Step 4 - confirm you answer

One of the biggest mistakes 80% of salespeople make when answering objections is they don't confirm their answers. In other words, they just keep talking past the close. The top 20% understand the danger of talking past the close (like introducing new objections). Instead, by using a scripted response they confirm their answer. Use any one of the following:

"Does that answer that for you?"

"Does that make sense?"

"Have I satisfied that for you?"

Step 5 - ask for the deal

This might sound obvious, but you'd be amazed by how many (like 80% or more) salespeople fail to ask for the deal. Scripts assure that you do. And after you ask for the order, shut up and listen!

The Top Seven Objections

The interesting thing about sales objections is that they are all basically the same. Regardless of what product or service you are selling, you will almost always get the same objections.

The secret of the top 20%? They are prepared for these common objections and have scripted effective rebuttals that they use each time they get them. When you combine this with the Five-Step Method for Handling Objections, you catapult yourself into the top 20% and often into the top 5%. Here are scripted responses that work (adapt, adjust and rewrite them to fit your product or service):

> The biggest mistake in closing is not asking for the sale.

I need to show this to my (partner, boss, etc.)

The first thing to do with this and other objections is to make sure it is a *real* objection and not a smokescreen or a put off. Do this by isolating and questioning the objection first. Listen completely to what your prospect says and then respond with:

> *"That is perfectly fine, _____. I think you should show this to (whomever they claim they need to show this to). And let me ask you something – if after you show this to _____, he/she says 'It looks good _____, whatever you want to do,' is this something that YOU would move forward with today?"*

Now be aware that any answer other than yes means that this objection is just a smokescreen and you haven't uncovered the real objection. You will have to keep qualifying. On the other hand, if your prospect says he would move forward on this today, confirm this and make him your ally. Say:

> *"Great, then I take it you are going to recommend this to _____, right? Wonderful! What can WE do to make sure*

he agrees with us?"

This is how to make your prospect an ally - you are now on the same team. Listen carefully to what your prospect says. If they are truly sold on your solution, they will tell you what you need to do to close the sale. Offer to do a three-way conference call, or to call and speak to the real decision maker directly. Ask about specific follow-up times or for additional information that you can provide them with. And always ask what the next step will be and agree on a time frame for follow up.

> Prepare for the most common objections in advance.

The bottom line is, when you get an objection it is either the real objection or a smokescreen, which is why it is critical to always qualify objections before answering them.

The price is too high (part one)

The price is too high is a favorite way for prospects to put off making a decision. The *price is too high* objection can have several meanings. It may mean that your prospect really can't afford your product or service, they may be able to get it cheaper somewhere else, or (more likely) they are not convinced of or don't understand the value of your offering.

Remember that a price question and a price objection are two different things. So for a price objection you must first qualify before you answer. Here is how you do it:

> *"I understand _____, and let me ask you a question. If price weren't an issue on this, would you move on this today and place an order with me?"*

Any answer other than *yes* means that it is a

smokescreen and not the real objection. If that is the case, then it is up to you to do more probing to uncover the real objection. If they say yes, however, it is time to close. Follow a *yes* answer with:

> *"Where does our price need to be for you to place an order with me today?"*

If your prospect gives you a price that is reasonable and one that you can match, then before you just lower your price, get your prospect to commit first. Say:

> *"OK _____. That price may or may not be something I can match. I'll have to speak to my manager about this. I'd be glad to do that, but before I do let me ask you again, if he says that I can get you the (repeat the size of the order and the price here) is this something you will move on today?"*

Only after they agree to move forward are you to put your prospect on hold and get the proper price approval. After you've gotten the approval, come back on the line and say:

> *"I'm happy to tell you that we can move ahead with this today. I know you'll be happy with this, and here's what we need to do to get you started . . .," Then close the sale.*

Of course, if they give you an unreasonable figure, one that you could never match, then you may have a non-buyer on your hands. Unreasonable price demands usually indicate that the prospect wasn't real to begin with. It means that next time you must practice better qualifying techniques.

The price is too high (part two)
Sometimes you will isolate and deal with the price

objection, only for it to come back again. If your price is in the ballpark but you are not the least expensive in town, build value. Here's how:

> *"I'm sure you know the old saying that 'you get what you pay for,' right? Well _____, you are right, we're not the cheapest in town, but I can guarantee you that you will get what you pay for with us."*

> *"You see, the most important reason for moving ahead with our product and my company today is the follow-up service you will get from me. _____, I pride myself on my client satisfaction, and I will always make myself available to you, and if I can't help you immediately, then I will find someone who can. You see the type of service I provide can't be bought at any price! I know you will always be glad you took action today, so let's get you started. Do you need a P.O. number on this or do I just make it to your attention?"*

You will be surprised by how successful this close is. Most of the time your prospect is just waiting for a reason to buy, and when you give it to them the deal gets done.

I want to think about it (part one)

"I want to think about it," is a tough objection to overcome because the prospect isn't saying never, they are just saying not now (unfortunately they really mean not now and not ever). The top 20% know that the best way to respond is with a rebuttal that gets the prospect to keep talking and reveal their real objection. The best way to respond is:

> *"That's perfectly OK, and I want you to think about it carefully before you make any decision. From what we have discussed so far, I know you understand how the (product or service) works right?"*

"And I know that if you were to decide to move ahead on this then the money wouldn't be a problem, I mean this does fit within your budget (whatever the amount is) today right?"

"And I know that you see the benefit of taking advantage of this (list a benefit that you know your prospect is interested in) today right?"

"Great! _____, just to clarify my thinking what part of the (product or service) is it that you want to think about?"

Now listen closely to what the prospect tells you. After you are clear on their answer, isolate and question it so you can uncover the real objection.

Another simple way to get your prospect to identify what is holding them back when they say, *"I want to think about it,"* is to simply say:

"_____, when I tell someone, 'I want to think about it,' it either means that I don't understand it or I'm not sold yet. Which is it for you?"

Listen carefully to what your prospect tells you and then isolate and question what they say to make sure it is the real objection.

I already have a supplier or company I work with

This is actually a great objection to get because it means you are talking to a buyer of the products or services you offer. Before you answer this objection, it is crucial to understand the relationship they have with their current vendor. You will want to know how the relationship began, what they like and don't like about it, and how they go about reviewing other potential vendors. As always, isolate the objection before proceeding. Start with:

"_____, I'm glad you're using the XYZ company for this. You see, I only work with companies who understand the importance of this service – my job is in increasing value not in introducing new accounts to this market. And ____, I'm sure the XYZ company is the best supplier you've found so far and that's why you are still using them, right?"

"Well _____, I'm interested in helping you take your business to the next level of (performance, service or value), and I want to start slowly with you and prove our worth. I don't expect a total switch, rather just an opportunity to help you improve your business. I'm going to suggest you start small with our (trial/demo product), and you'll then have a chance to compare our (product, service, performance) side-by-side. After 90 days, you be the judge. Now I can have this out to you by next Tuesday or would Thursday be better for you?"

If your prospect still says no, ask them how they got started with their current supplier, and ask them for the same opportunity to earn their business.

We don't have the budget

Sometimes even when you qualify for budget you still get this objection when you ask for the order. About half the time it is a real objection, and the other half of the time it is a stall. The good news is that there are several effective ways for dealing with it. The most important thing to say in response to this objection is:

"_____, if the budget were available on this, would you move forward on it today?"

Now listen carefully. Any hesitation or answer other than a *yes* means that budget is not the real or complete objection and you need to dig deeper. Use these probing questions:

"What else is important here?"

"What else would you need to see before you would move forward with this?"

If your prospect says they would move forward if they had the budget, then it's time for you to get creative and help your prospect *find* the budget. Good questions to use to help your prospect find or create the needed budget include:

"What do you usually do when an emergency expenditure comes up – where do you get the budget for that?"

You will be surprised what resources your prospect can come up with if you let them. Remember to listen! Also try:

"Who else could you go to, to get approval to go beyond the budget for this?"

"When was the last time you were able to squeeze something like this into your budget?"

"Well _____, since you do agree that this solution would be a perfect fit for you, where could you get the money from?"

"_____, if I could structure the payments on this to fit within your current budget and spread the other payments into your next budget period, would that make it easier to get started with this today?"

Listen to each response, continue to question and probe, and then ask for the order.

I want to think about it (part two)

Sometimes at the end of your presentation you will still get, *"I want to think about it."* An excellent means of dealing with this objection is using a technique that will often get your prospect to tell you their real concern. If your prospect tells you that they still want to think about it, just say:

> *"You know _____, I understand. I know I've given you a lot of information, and some clients I speak with tell me the same thing. I'm concerned that I may have stressed the (now pick a part of your presentation that is pretty straight forward, like the warranty or return policy) a little too much, what do you think?"*

And then shut up and listen. In many cases your prospect will correct you and reveal their real reason for not moving forward. If for some reason you are still not clear, simply respond with an occasional, *"Oh?"* or *"What do you mean?"* to keep them talking. This is the time to let your prospect speak and to give them plenty of opportunities to do so. If you use these techniques and remain quiet, you'll be surprised by how many times your prospect will reveal their real objection.

Stop Talking Past the Close

Talking past the close is common. You deliver a great presentation, think that your prospect is with you, but you just keep talking. You know you should stop but you don't. It has happened to all of us. Other than not asking for the business, this is the biggest closing mistake made in sales. The reason so many salespeople talk past the close is because it is risky to ask for the deal and face rejection. It's much easier to keep talking. Unfortunately when this happens, salespeople end up talking their prospect out of the sale or muddy the water by introducing new objections. Here are five ways to stop talking past the close:

> Talking past the close is the second biggest mistake made in closing.

Record yourself

I've said this before, and here it comes again. Record yourself and listen to your calls. The best way to break *habitual deal killing* is to hear yourself do it.

Use a script

One of the best parts of a well-crafted script is that it ends with you asking for the deal. Practice and stick to your scripts.

Ask for the deal five times

Make a commitment to yourself to ask for the deal at least five times during the close. Make a game of it and keep track of your score.

Welcome "no"

Getting a *no* stinks. Which is why so many sales reps avoid *no's* like the plague. However, in sales *no* is a fact of life and to climb into the top 20% you must become comfortable getting and dealing with *no*. Re-frame the way you think about *no*. Realize the truth, even if it sounds like a cliche, each *no* gets you closer to a *yes*. Some sales professionals even count *no's* and try to rack up as many as possible - knowing, of course that more *no's* equal more *yeses*. So welcome getting a *no*. It means you are that much closer to getting the sale.

Shut up and listen

Force yourself to be quiet after you ask for the sale. Use your mute button or cover the mouthpiece and count to three – 1001, 1002, 1003. By forcing yourself to remain silent for three seconds after asking for the sale, you will have something to concentrate on other than fear. This may sound silly, but it works – try it.

The bottom line is that the top 20% know the value of asking for the sale and remaining silent.

Real Secrets

- **The top 20% don't answer objections - they isolate and question them.**

- **Use the Five-Step Method to effectively handle objections.**

- **Prepare and use scripts for the top seven most common objections.**

- **Stop talking past the close.**

- **The top 20% ask for the sale and remain silent.**

6 | *Expect To Win*

What do the top salespeople, top athletes, top performers, and top business people all have in common? A winning attitude. Winners expect and insist on success.

In sales, when a top 20% producer goes into a close, they expect to get the sale no matter what.

They know it might be hard, and that there will be objections, but they believe with certainty that the deal will close.

Their attitude is that if anyone can get the deal done, they can. It is this attitude that gives them the ability to stay in the close longer and draw upon more of their skills, knowledge, and talent, because they see themselves winning.

It is like them to keep asking for the order. It is like them to make five, ten, or fifteen thousand dollars a month and more. It is like them to be a top 20% producer. That is their attitude, their belief about themselves; and, like all of us, they will always act according to their self-image.

If you want to become one of the top producers in your company or industry, you will first have to develop a top 20% attitude. It will not help to learn a lot of new skills and then go out and try to change your old behavior or habits if you still think in the same old way. Your self-talk always reinforces the dominant belief you have of yourself. It always reinforces the picture of how you see yourself behaving and performing. If you don't change your internal beliefs and thoughts, then as soon as you get objections, or get blown off, or miss a sale, your old self-talk will come in to bring you back down to where you "really see yourself." You will hear yourself saying things like:

> Pay attention to your self-talk - all long lasting change starts on the inside and works its way out.

"Oh this stuff doesn't work" or,

"I knew I wouldn't get that sale" or,

"See, this always happens; I never do this right."

Before you know it, you will go back to your old habits, and you will get your old results. This is one of the most important things you will ever learn: *All long lasting, permanent change starts first on the inside and works its way out.* These changes include your self-image or picture of yourself, your self-talk, your beliefs, your subconscious mind, and your goals.

A Positive Self-image

We all have a mental picture of how we see ourselves acting or performing. We see ourselves as shy or outgoing, dynamic or boring, a good closer or a bad closer, good at questioning prospects or bad at it, patient or always in a rush, thin or always needing to go on a diet, a reader or someone who prefers to watch TV, and so on.

The pictures we have are rarely neutral - we are either good at one thing, or not so good at another. This collection of attitudes and beliefs about ourselves is what is called our self-image.

Now here's the important thing, so read carefully: *Your self-image (the picture you have of yourself) will always determine your results.* It doesn't matter how much you know and it does not matter how much desire or motivation you have, the real regulator of your performance is and always will be your self-image in any particular area.

You can see the power of self-image in the top 20%. You can see it in their work habits. They are usually the ones who make the most number of cold calls. They are the ones who will use five, eight or even fifteen closes if necessary, - anything it takes to get the sale. And if for some reason they miss a sale, their self-talk is positive. They will say to themselves:

"That wasn't like me" or,
"Next time I will do better" or,
"I may not have gotten that sale, but I learned on that call and my next call will go so much better as a result"

Everything they feed themselves corresponds with their successful self-image and perpetuates it. The point is that the way you build, support or change your self-image will have a direct impact on who you become and what you accomplish.

Positive Self-talk

There is a constant stream of internal dialogue going on in our heads during every waking moment of the day. Researchers say that on average we have over 60,000 thoughts a day, and these thoughts come to us in the form of self-talk. The important thing is this: *It is your self-talk that continually forms, shapes, and reinforces your self-image.*

If you want to change your results, you must first change your self-image and that means changing your self-talk. Unfortunately, the problem for most of us is, we are not really aware of what we are saying to ourselves. Most people who stop and really listen to their self-talk are surprised at how negative and self-defeating it is. Have you ever heard yourself saying any of the following:

"I can't afford that" or,
"How am I going to pay my bills" or,
"I never get that kind of sale" or,
"Oh, I just knew they weren't going to buy."

By continually thinking negative thoughts you are in effect attracting negative outcomes. It is self-defeating to feed yourself the things you don't want to happen. Negative self-talk like this constantly builds the self-image or picture of an underachiever.

What does your self-talk sound like? What are you feeding yourself? Do your thoughts support you in making sales or do they instill fear and uncertainty while you are trying to close? Do they lift you up or tear you down? Do they launch you into the future or mire you in the past? Are you spending the majority of your energy worrying about what won't work for you, how you never have enough money, or never enough time, etc? Or, are you dwelling on what will work and how great it is going to be once you have achieved your goal?

The first step in building a winning attitude is to listen to your self-talk and begin making positive changes. Once you become consciously aware of your self-image and how you are constantly feeding and building it, you will then be in a position to change it.

Manage Your Subconscious Mind

Your subconscious mind is the part of you that is always listening to your every thought, is blindly accepting your every wish and pronouncement, and is constantly and creatively producing in your outer world everything that you believe to be true in your inner world. Its job is to make your outer world look like your inner picture.

One of the most amazing features of your subconscious is its inability to tell the difference between true and false. Whatever you feel is true, becomes true for you. So when you constantly affirm that you never make sales on Fridays, or that you are just not that good at cold calling, or that you never have enough money, you are automatically, in advance, creating in your life exactly the results and circumstances you don't want!

> Your subconscious mind makes your outer world conform to your inner picture.

The key to success in all areas of your life is to get the picture of how you want your life to be, of how you want to see yourself acting, into your subconscious mind first. It will do the rest. Just as it is doing now and has been doing all along; it will work day and night to make your outer world mirror your inner world.

In fact, if you want to know what you have been feeding it for the last three months, just look at your life today. What is your income level like? Where do you live? What kind of car do you drive? How is your relationship with your significant other? You have a distinct picture about these and all other areas of your life, and you have been

> Affirmations help you shape your internal picture of yourself.

building and feeding this picture to your subconscious mind through your self-talk. Your subconscious mind, being your obedient servant, has faithfully created your life to match this picture. To give you some idea of how your subconscious mind works, imagine if it wrote you a letter:

Dear you,

I do your every bidding; I ask no questions. I accept as fact whatever you feel is true. I do not presume to change anything you think, feel, say, or do.

I remember everything and file it away in perfect order, quickly and efficiently, and then I return it to you exactly as you gave it to me.

I am the reservoir of your deepest, most heartfelt desires and, one way or another, I see to it that you get what you really want. I am with you always and I never sleep; nothing can impede my activity.

Do not presume to limit me with restrictions of time and space. Time and space mean nothing to me; I always exist in the here and now.

In fulfilling your wishes, remember I have infinite power and resources at my disposal.

I am your humble, obedient, and masterfully efficient servant; I implement your every command without hesitation or criticism.

To get the best results, always communicate with me in my native tongue: The language of pictures, symbols, and images.

I cooperate fully when you feel or say you are "this" or, "that," and I faithfully see to it that your every expectation is fulfilled.

I do not argue, judge, analyze, question, or make decisions; I accept all impressions easily and readily, and then I set upon them. My forte is deductive reasoning, memory, and association.

I work on everything you give me, and I creatively expand all of your feelings and ideas. I then express and manifest all possible conclusions and results of what you think and feel, insofar as the circumstances of your life permit me to do so.

I take everything you hold inside of you and project it out, therefore, the world you see is what you are. Always remember, I rely on your discrimination, and I respond to your choices and decisions.

Sincerely yours,
Your subconscious mind

Your subconscious mind is responsible for acting on the pictures and thoughts you feed it. And the best way to change your thoughts is with affirmations and goals.

The Power of Affirmations

Affirmations are nothing more than positive self-talk. Since you are already talking to yourself at a rate of 60,000 thoughts a day, and since your subconscious mind is going to believe and act on these thoughts anyway, doesn't it make sense to take control of your self-talk and begin creating the results you really want? The best way to do this is with positive affirmations.

Positive affirmations should be made up of short

sentences, or paragraphs that fit onto an index card. I like using index cards because they are easy to carry with me. When writing your affirmations, you should always keep them in the first person such as, *"I am a consistent and effective closer,"* or, *"I enjoy cashing my $2,000 pay checks each week."*

Keep your affirmations in the present tense, *as if you already have the result you desire.* Notice I didn't say that I am *going* to be, or that it will be nice *when* I . . . For affirmations to be the most effective, they should be in the first person, as if you are already enjoying the new behavior you desire. Remember, your subconscious cannot tell the difference between true and false.

Some people object to affirmations because they feel they are lying to themselves. Not true! You are simply taking conscious control of your subconscious. Of course you can always continue feeding yourself negative thoughts that produce circumstances and results in your life that you don't want. It is your choice.

To develop positive affirmations, begin by listening to the negative affirmations that you are habitually saying now. You will be surprised at the number and frequency of the negative statements that are shaping your life.

Once you have identified these negative statements, write positive opposites. For example, if after you lose a sale you are in the habit of saying, *"See I just knew they weren't going to buy,"* change it to, *"I really did my best on that close and boy did I sound good. The next person who hears me deliver a presentation that well, will definitely buy!"* Imagine how much confidence and enthusiasm you will have for your next close if you just change your self-talk like that.

> The most powerful source of positive and effective affirmations are your goals.

Affirmations should be used in all areas of your life. By writing them down on index cards, you will have instant access to them throughout your day. For the best results, take five to ten minutes three to five times a day and read and visualize them slowly to yourself. It is important to be relaxed when you read them, and to feel them with as much emotion as you can. It is your emotional involvement that will determine how much of an affect your new affirmations have in your life. This is an example of an affirmation card that I used to become a top 20% producer.

Front of Card

$55,000 GROSS PROFIT PRODUCTION
I feel so powerful now that I'm closing more business. It's like me to qualify each prospect thoroughly, and I often uncover their exact buying motives. I'm a powerful closer, and if my prospect says no, that's when I go to work—I listen for my opening, and then I use the right scripts, rebuttals, and closing techniques. And it's working! I'm closing more sales, making more money, and I love seeing my numbers go higher and higher! I knew I could do it!

Back of Card

$55,000 GROSS PROFIT PRODUCTION

PAY VALUE:
*Weekend getaways in Santa Barbara.
*Moving into my new home.
*Seeing that additional income in my check.
*Having that trophy on my desk all month.

Set Winning Goals

The most powerful source of positive and effective affirmations are your goals. Write affirmations that paint the picture of how good you will feel once you have accomplished those goals. Goal setting is one of the basic ingredients for success, and there are many great books and audio programs on proper goal setting techniques. *Zig Ziglar's Goals* and *Jeb Blount's PowerPrinciples* are two of my favorites. Invest in them! Goals are road maps to your success.

Do you have clearly defined, written goals that you review and revise often? A study of Harvard graduates showed that out of an entire graduating class, only 3% had clearly defined written down goals. Twenty years later a follow up study showed that the 3% that had written goals earned more as a group then did the other 97% combined. That's powerful! As the saying goes, if you don't know where you are going you will probably end up somewhere else.

To be a top 20% producer you must have goals. The way to start is to make a list of the things you want to have in your lifetime. The only rule is there are no limits. This is your time to dream big dreams. You can fill up a page or a notebook. The clearer you become the more effective your subconscious mind will be in bringing them into your life.

Another important consideration is to goal set in all areas of your life. You don't just want to have goals for your career, because you are more than just your profession. Create goals for your personal life, including your health, spirituality, and your relationships. Once you have made a list of your goals in each area of your life, break them down into 20 year , 10 year, 5 year, annual, quarterly, and finally daily goals.

Let's say for example that you have set a career goal of making $100,000 this year. First, realize that in order to reach this, your monthly income will be $8,333, or $2,083 a week, or

$416 a day. Next, figure out how many calls you need to make in a day to generate enough sales to create this level of income. Once you know the number of cold calls and closing calls you need to make on a daily, monthly, quarterly, and yearly basis, you will then be able to set goals that will produce the results you want.

> The most powerful force in your life is your power to choose.

And if you know that you need to make 100 cold calls a day to reach your goal, that will help you build your affirmation: *"I feel great making 100 cold calls a day. I feel powerful and confident as I accomplish my goal of earning $2,083 each week. I love going to the bank and cashing my...,"* and so on. Do you get the idea?

My challenge to you is to take control of your destiny and start consciously directing the outcomes you want. You do have a choice, so why not create the life you deserve?

How long does it take to produce results? Usually a minimum period of 30 days before you start to notice a change in your attitude and actions. But after that something magical will happen. You will start to think differently. You will start to expect different and better things in your life. Your confidence will grow, and, most importantly, your results will change. You will begin thinking and acting like a winner.

Decide exactly what it is that you want out of life, and make a commitment to get it. Life is not a dress rehearsal, this is it. Everything you want is just waiting for you to claim it!

The Power of Choice

You now have all the tools you need to double your income selling over the phone. Realize that some of these ideas may be new to you and therefore might take some time getting used to. Don't give up! By incorporating a few of these ideas and techniques into your life, little by little, they will soon become second nature to you. And by improving a little bit each day, you will find that over the coming months, you will improve a lot. And your results will reflect that.

Remember, success is not just one big, sudden thing. Success is a series of tiny steps that you take on a consistent basis. By improving a little every day you will find yourself moving toward the goals, and the future, that you have decided are right for you.

It is an incredible feeling. So make that commitment to yourself, and start today. Join the ranks of the top 20%, and begin enjoying the extra income, confidence, lifestyle, and peace of mind you deserve.

In this book I have given you all I have to give to help you become the best. I know that these concepts and techniques work because I have used them personally to improve my own life. I have taught thousands of other people who have in turn created the results that they, too, wanted in their lives. Now it is up to you. You have a choice, right now, to change your life, and to become a top 20% producer if you are willing to make the commitment.

Real Secrets

- All top performers have one thing in common - a winning attitude.

- All long lasting, permanent change starts first on the inside and works its way out.

- Your self-image is the real regulator of performance.

- To change your performance, change how you see yourself.

- Use affirmations to change your self-talk.

- Your subconscious mind believes whatever you feed it and will create your reality with that information.

- To move into the top 20% you must have goals.

- The power to change your life starts with a choice.

- Are you committed?

7 | *Bonus:*
The Next Level

If you are already in the top 20% of the producers in your company or industry, or when you join that elite group, it will be time for you to take the next step.

If you have already mastered the techniques discussed in this book, then I have some good news for you. You are ready to move into the top 1% of the top 20%.

The secret to moving into the top 1%, is to build a support staff of assistants, qualifiers, and dialers, so you can spend more time closing deals rather than prospecting for leads or dealing with all the paperwork that goes along with writing business.

Now I understand that not all sales positions offer the opportunity to build a private staff. However, if yours does, the following information can change your career and life. The point: *you can only make a sale when you are speaking with a qualified prospect asking for the order.* Your main focus should be structuring your entire working environment so that you are in the closing arena as much as possible. The

---

> The real secret of the top 1% is employing a support staff.

way to do this is to invest in and build a support staff within your company that is dedicated to helping you leverage your talents as a closer. While at first it may seem expensive to invest your time and money into building your own staff of people, experience proves that you can earn five to ten times more than you do today by getting others to help you. Here's how you do it:

There are three types of support staff you will need to help you accomplish this goal - dialers, qualifiers, and assistants. This sounds like a lot of people to hire, but the key is to start slowly and then build as your income increases. If you are working alone right now, the easiest and most cost effective way to begin building your support staff is by hiring a dialer.

Dialers

A dialer is a person whose job is to locate people for you to talk with. As you know from your own prospecting efforts, you spend a lot of your time just trying to reach people to qualify. Invariably, people are not home or in the office. Because of this you spend valuable closing time dialing just to reach someone to talk to.

This is why hiring a dialer is the perfect way to become more efficient. They do not try to qualify people, nor do they try to reestablish interest on a closing call. Their sole job is to call a prospect and make sure they are either at home or in the office.

Your dialer should be near you, or at least have the ability to transfer calls to you easily. When they find someone who is at home or in the office, they should simply say,

"Hello, my name is _____, and I am calling from the office of _____ at the ABC company. Please hold for Mr./Mrs. _____."

Then your dialer will hand off the call to you. Remember, sales is still a numbers game, and the more people you reach in a day the more successful you are going to be. If you are on the phone when your dialer reaches someone, they would simply say:

"Hello, my name is _____, and I am calling from the office of Mr./Mrs. _____ at the ABC company. Mr./Mrs. _____ needs to have quick word with you but I see that he/she has just picked up the other phone. Are you going to be available for the next ½ hour?"

At this point your prospect will want to know what is going on. If your prospect asks what this call is about, have your dialer simply respond:

"It is regarding (state a benefit of the) ABC company. Mr./Mrs. _____ wanted me to get you on the phone. I will make sure and have him/her get right back to you. Thank you."

As your dialer works through the leads you give them, they will accumulate a list of people who are available, know your name, and are expecting to hear from you. By utilizing a dialer properly, you will eliminate much of the unproductive time you are now spending trying to reach people to speak with. Imagine the benefits you will gain by having a stack of leads that you know you will be able to reach at almost any time. It is a very inexpensive way to become more efficient.

Some of the best dialers I have hired have been high

school kids. High school kids tend to be hard working, will gladly work for minimum wage, and usually know a lot of other kids you can hire as you grow.

Qualifiers

After you are successfully working with dialers, you will find that you have more people to reach than you can handle. Not a bad position to be in. What you now want to do is hire a person who's main responsibility is to qualify those prospects for you. They will have to be trained to read a qualifying script, ask all the appropriate qualifying questions, and then determine whether or not information should be sent out to that particular prospect.

The goal of your qualifier is to provide you with prospects that have already been qualified and are ready for you to close. In other words, your qualifier should hand you a list of qualified prospects each day that are ready to go.

The qualifier's job is more complex than the dialer's, which means you will have to spend more time training and working with them at first. You will want them to qualify just as you would, and you will want them to be just as discerning as you would be. But the rewards will far exceed the initial investment in training.

The key to getting a good qualifier is to hire the right person. There are several ways to find good qualifiers. The first way is to promote one of your dialers. Here you have someone who already knows your product, knows your company, and knows the way you do business. If you find that you have a really hard worker who wants to succeed in the business, then seriously consider promoting them.

Another way is to run an ad. You can post jobs free online on websites like Craigslist.com and SalesGravy.com. If you run your ad in the newspaper, place the ad in the sales section rather than the telemarketing section. You will get a larger response rate. In your ad stress that you are offering not just a job, but an opportunity to learn a new career or skill. A sample ad might read:

SALES ASSISTANT WANTED
Energetic, enthusiastic, self-starter wanted
to assist top broker. Earn while
you learn to be the best with our top training
program. Excellent opportunity for high pay
and advancement. Call now for your
confidential interview.

You will be amazed by how many people will respond to an ad like this. The person you are looking for will either have experience or is someone who is enthusiastic, aggressive, and has good communication skills.

When considering how much you are going to pay a qualifier there are several things to consider. First, you want to avoid hiring someone who sounds good on the interview only to find out after two or three weeks that you have made a mistake. The way to avoid this is to give your potential qualifier a two week trial period during which you make it clear to them that they are trying out for the job.

In the trial period pay them a minimum wage or close to it with the understanding that if they work out, the salary and commission will be adjusted to a previously agreed upon amount. This will give you the time to judge their performance before committing yourself.

In addition, it is very important to pay a small base salary combined with a sliding scale commission. Everyone works harder when on commission. Your qualifier should feel that the amount of money they make is directly related to the results they

> A qualifier frees you up to spend 90% of your time closing.

produce. You must remember that your goal is to stay in the closing arena as much as possible. Your ideal day should consist of nothing but making closing presentations to qualified prospects. Keep the goal of being in the closing arena foremost in your mind as you build your dynasty!

Secretaries and assistants

When you add your own secretary (or personal assistant) to your staff, you will finally be free to do nothing but close. Your assistant's job will be to handle all your call-ins, handle all your paperwork, take care of all your correspondence, and even help with some of your personal obligations.

This person will also handle payroll for your staff, and manage and supervise their efforts. Here again it is a good idea to search through your current staff of dialers and qualifiers to look for a top personal assistant. You want someone who is familiar with your operation or industry and someone who has had experience in managing others.

You can of course run an ad for a secretary or assistant, and again I suggest the two week training period so that you can see first hand if they have what it takes to handle the pressure. Unlike your dialers and qualifiers, however, your assistant will be on straight salary. Check to see what the normal salary is for the secretaries in your office now and use that as a guideline. Start with the lowest salary at first with the understanding that pay will increase as performance increases. Remember, you can always raise a salary but never lower it.

> Assistants remove the burden of paperwork and other menial tasks.

You may be thinking that this is sounding like a very elaborate and expensive proposition. I admit that once you get to the point of having one or two dialers, three or four qualifiers and a secretary, you will indeed be spending money to keep it going. But at that point you will be making five to ten times more money than you ever dreamed of and it won't matter!

You have to realize that nobody ever made a lot of money working alone. You can only do so much on your own. If you truly want to move into the elite top 1%, you are going to have to rely on others to do menial and time consuming things that take your focus away from the only thing that makes you money - closing. How big your staff becomes will be determined by a number of things such as your ability to close, your commitment to be the best, and your goals and limitations.

Conclusion

We have covered a lot of ground, all designed to help you close more sales over the phone. A word of caution though: *these skills and techniques will only work if you use them.* It is up to you to apply, practice, and incorporate these skills into your daily routine. At first these techniques may seem a little awkward, but with practice you will find yourself improving more quickly than you ever thought possible.

My goal with this book is not just to provide you with the tools and techniques of the top 20%. More important than that, I want to challenge you to commit to becoming the absolute best in the profession of sales. I know from experience that if you make this commitment to yourself, your family, and your profession, that you will soon join the top 20%. I wish you the best and will see you at the top!

Real Secrets

- **Move into the top 1% of the top 20% by building a support staff.**

- **Dialers help you become more efficient at finding prospects to talk to.**

- **Qualifiers ensure that each day you have a stack of prospects to close.**

- **Personal assistants free you from paperwork and menial chores.**

- **Your staff will always work harder when they are paid commission.**

- **The key to success with your support staff is finding and hiring the right people.**

- **When you spend 90% of your time closing your income will increase by 5 to 10 times.**

- **The power to change your life starts with a choice.**

- **Are you committed?**

Mike Brooks is founder and principle of Mr Inside Sales, a Los Angeles based Inside Sales and Telesales consulting and training firm. He publishes an internationally acclaimed free weekly ezine called, "Secrets of the Top 20%", works with companies as an executive coach, and as a sales trainer teaching the skills, techniques and habits of top 20% sales performers. He specializes in working with under-performing outbound or inbound inside sales teams.

Mike started his career in the financial and securities industry as an investment broker, and quickly became the top producer out of five branch offices in Southern California. Promoted to Executive Vice President of Sales, he developed a Top 20% Inside Sales Training Program that doubled corporate sales of private placements from $27 million a year to over $58 million and then doubled it again the following year to over $112 million.

Since that time Mike has consulted with sales organizations across many different industries. His experience has proven that the 80/20 rule applies regardless of industry and, moreover, that once sales teams learn and apply proven Top 20% techniques and strategies, their sales performance (and morale) immediately improves.

If you're interested in having Mr Inside Sales conduct in *in-house customized training* or speak at your next sales convention, visit his website: *www.MrInsideSales.com.* Contact Mike directly by email: *Mike@MrInsideSales.com*

Acknowledgements

This book has been a long time in the making, and I owe a debt of gratitude to the many people who have made it possible to produce. To begin with, I want to acknowledge and thank my very first sales manager, Peter Brooks, my brother, who taught me all those years ago the importance of listening. I can still see him standing next to me holding his hand out like a stop sign right as I was about to begin talking over my prospect.

Next I want to acknowledge and thank my publisher, Jeb Blount, and his team at Sales Gravy Press for the many hours (days and weeks!) they have invested in reading, revising and reshaping this manuscript and turning it into the polished book you have in your hands now. I can't tell you how much your dedication and hard work has meant to me – Thank You!!

And, a big thank you to my many friends who reviewed the manuscript and provided valuable feedback. I especially want to thank Jill Konrath, Lee Salz, Michael Day, Carrie Blount, Wendy Weiss, Karl Goldfield, and April Canada. I am deeply touched that you took time from your busy schedules to help me.

Also, I want to thank all those sales reps who I have had the honor to work with through the years. It is your willingness to learn and apply new techniques, and your desire to be the best that has inspired me to give my best also. It has been a pleasure to help you grow, and the benefit is that I get to keep growing as well.

I'd also like to acknowledge the entrepreneurial business owners who have hired me to come in and help them grow a successful sales force. It is your continuing belief that things could and should be better that has allowed me the opportunity to work with some of the greatest sales teams in the country.

Finally, I'd like to thank my mentor, Stan Billue, who all those years ago challenged me to be the best me I could become.

LaVergne, TN USA
23 December 2010
209945LV00001B/144/P